בס"ד

Links in the Chassidic Legacy

Biographical Sketches
that First Appeared in the
Classic Columns of *HaTamim*

Translated by Shimon Neubort

SICHOS IN ENGLISH
788 EASTERN PARKWAY
BROOKLYN, NEW YORK 11213

5757•1997

LINKS IN THE CHASSIDIC LEGACY

PUBLISHED AND COPYRIGHTED © BY
SICHOS IN ENGLISH
788 EASTERN PARKWAY • BROOKLYN, N.Y. 11213
TEL. (718) 778-5436

ALL RIGHTS RESERVED. NO PART OF THIS PUBLICATION MAY
BE REPRODUCED IN ANY FORM OR BY ANY MEANS,
INCLUDING PHOTO-COPYING, WITHOUT PERMISSION IN
WRITING FROM THE COPYRIGHT HOLDER OR THE PUBLISHER.

ISBN 1-8814-0023-9

1ST PRINTING 5757 • 1997
2ND PRINTING 5760 • 1999

Library of Congress Catalogue Information
Title: Links in the chassidic legacy ; biographical sketches that first appeared in the classic columns of *HaTamim* / translated by Shimon Neubort.
Published: Brooklyn, N.Y.: Sichos In English, 1997
Description: xiv, 209 p.; 24 cm.
LC Call No.: BM750.L56 1997
Dewey No.: 296.8/332/0922 B 21
ISBN: 1881400239
Subjects: Hasidim -- Biography. Habad.
Other authors: Schneersohn, Joseph Isaac, 1880-1950.
Neubort, Shimon.
Other titles: Tamim.
Control No.: 971-41956 // r97

Table of Contents

Translator's Introduction V
Editor's Jottings XI
Introduction by the Editors of *HaTamim* XIV
Rashbatz 1
Reb Chanoch Hendel 37
Reb Avraham Ber 43
Reb "Y.M." 65
Rashdam 93
Reb Chayim Yehoshua 105
Reb Gavriel *Nossai Chein* 113
The Vilenker Brothers 125
Reb Avraham Abba Persan 131
Typical Chassidic Businessmen:
    Reb Michoel Aharon Pisarevsky and Reb Leib Posen . 137
    Reb Meir Mordechai Czernin 155
Reb Yitzchak the Tailor's Father 157
Appendix
    A: Letter from the Rebbe Maharash 175
    B: Letter from the *Tzemach Tzedek* 181
    C: Chassidic Discourse on the Subject of "Shining" .. 189
    D: Early History of *Yeshivah Tomchei Temimim* 192
Founders of Chassidism & Leaders of *Chabad*-Lubavitch .. 197
Glossary 198

Translator's Introduction

The original *Yeshivah Tomchei Temimim* Lubavitch was established by the Rebbe Rashab in the summer of 1897, in the village of Lubavitch itself. The Rebbe Rashab was forced to leave Lubavitch in 1915; about two years later, the central *yeshivah* was disbanded, and the *Temimim* went into exile. Various branches were established throughout Russia and the Ukraine, and eventually the central *yeshivah* was also reestablished in Rostov, where the Rebbe Rayatz was then living (the Rebbe Rashab passed away in Rostov in 1920), and later in Leningrad.

The Rebbe Rayatz left the Soviet Union in 1927, living first in Riga and then in Warsaw. When the central *yeshivah* was established in Warsaw, many young students of Polish and Lithuanian *yeshivos* — who had become attracted by the Lubavitcher Rebbe's emissaries and by the *Chabad* style of *avodah* — came to study in its halls. They joined the few Soviet refugees of the earlier *yeshivos* who had managed to escape to Poland.

Thus, the pre-World War II *Temimim* fell into four categories: i) the original *Temimim* who had studied in Lubavitch under the Rebbe Rashab; ii) the students who had studied in Rostov or (later) in Leningrad under the Rebbe Rayatz; iii) the students of "Lubavitch-in-Exile," who had studied in the various Soviet branches, most of whom had never met the Previous Rebbe; iv) the "Polish" students of the *yeshivah* in Warsaw (and later, Otwock, a suburb of Warsaw).

In 1930's Warsaw, the Students' Organization of *Yeshivah Tomchei Temimim* carried on regular and extensive correspondence with students and alumni throughout Poland, with those still in the Soviet Union with whom correspondence was possible, and with those who had emigrated to the United States, Canada, Israel, and elsewhere.

The periodical *HaTamim* was published in Warsaw by the Students' Organization of *Yeshivah Tomchei Temimim* Lubavitch, during the period Tammuz 5695-Kislev 5698 (July 1935-December 1937). Besides sections devoted to *Toras HaChassidus* and to the revealed aspects of Torah, *HaTamim* regularly featured a section called "History of the Chassidim," devoted to biographical sketches of "famous chassidic personalities" in the history of *Chabad Chassidus*.

Many articles in this series of *HaTamim* do not bear the name of a specific author. However, elder chassidim who were students in the *yeshivah* at that time, have assured me that several of these articles were either authored by the Rebbe Rayatz, or compiled from his notes, diary, and letters. "For certain reasons" (which they declined to discuss), the Rebbe's authorship was not acknowledged in print. But those who are familiar with the Previous Rebbe's unique narrative style will recognize that same style in much of this writing.

Only eight issues of *HaTamim* were published; material was collected, and work was begun, for Issue No 9, but the impending outbreak of World War II prevented publication. *Yeshivah Tomchei Temimim* of Warsaw was disbanded, and its students went into exile, many of them in the Far East. Other Polish students escaped to the eastern republics of the Soviet Union, where they were united with their brethren of the Russian and Ukrainian branches.

The *Temimim* who (with G-d's help) managed to survive the war, remained scattered afterward. Some of them were trapped in the Soviet Union for decades. The Previous

Rebbe, after his escape from Warsaw on the eve of the Nazi invasion, settled in the Crown Heights section of Brooklyn. There, the central *Yeshivah Tomchei Temimim* was reestablished. Unfortunately, publication of *HaTamim* was never resumed, and the final story in this series remained unfinished. This material was subsequently discovered in the Previous Rebbe's library.

When I first came to "Seven-Seventy" thirty-five years ago, the purpose of my coming was (of course) to see and hear the Rebbe. But the Rebbe could be seen only during the formal public prayer services, and he could be heard only at the (in those days) monthly *farbrengens*. And being admitted to his holy presence for *yechidus* was a very rare privilege. But, as the Rebbe instructed us explicitly, we sought supplementary sources of inspiration and guidance.

At that time, numerous elder chassidim of the original *Temimim* were still living. Some lived in Crown Heights, and I had the opportunity to see them regularly, engage them in conversation, observe their *davening*, and listen to their stories and *farbrengens*. Others lived elsewhere in the United States and Canada, and would come to 770 to be with the Rebbe for festivals and other special occasions. Some lived in Europe and Israel, and would come only once a year (or less frequently), usually during the month of *Tishrei*.

During a *farbrengen* — or even a casual conversation — with these elder *Temimim*, you could catch a glimpse of Lubavitch as it had once been. They told stories of the Rebbeim of old that they had personally witnessed, or that they had heard from elder chassidim during their own youth.

To us American youngsters, the idea of *mesirus nefesh* was somewhat foreign; our greatest trials consisted of such things as getting up in time for *Kerias Shema* after a late night *farbrengen*, the occasional dip in an icy ritual bath (because someone had forgotten to turn on the heat), or traveling to some far-away place in summertime, to do Lubavitch outreach work, on a bus that lacked air conditioning.

Now, we met chassidim whose *mesirus nefesh* was on another plane entirely. Many had risked torture and death at the hands of the agents of the Czar, and later, Stalin's agents and the *Yevsektzia*. Some had suffered poverty and hunger. Many had suffered ridicule and beatings. Others had suffered disinheritance by their families, and were shunned by friends and neighbors, simply for the "crime" of adopting and disseminating the chassidic way of life. The Rebbe became their father, and Lubavitch became their mother.

Listening to these elders tell of their own experiences, and those of their companions and their own mentors, gave us some insight into how great *Chassidus* really is, and what a long way we still had to go before we could call ourselves chassidim.

But who were the "elders" that these original *Temimim* had looked up to? Who had inspired *them*, when they were youngsters? Before there was a formal *yeshivah* in Lubavitch, there had been the "sitters": advanced students who had come to Liozna, then to Liadi, then to Lubavitch, to pursue advanced study while basking in the glory of the Holy of Holies, the Alter Rebbe, the Mitteler, Rebbe, the *Tzemach Tzedek* and the Rebbe Maharash. They then became the *mashpiyim* of succeeding generations. In these pages, we find the stories of a few of those "famous chassidic personalities."

Many disciples of these earlier *mashpiyim* went on to become *mashpiyim* themselves, and developed their own disciples. But by no means all of them — not everyone is suited by nature, aptitude, or inclination to become a *mashpia*, *Rav*, *rosh yeshivah*, *mashgiach*, or even a *shochet*. Some remained private citizens — ordinary chassidic Jews — who combined their business activities or manual labor with Torah study, worship of the Creator, and intense love of their fellow Jews, all in the chassidic style. In these pages, we find a few of these "typical chassidic businessmen" too.

The present English translation was originally published in my weekly column "Biographical Sketches," in *Beis Moshiach* Magazine. It follows in the same spirit as our earlier translation of the Previous Rebbe's historical and biographical narrative, *The Making of* Chassidim. Once again, I wish to express my gratitude to the editors, publishers, and especially the readers of *Beis Moshiach* Magazine for their constant help and encouragement.

I am grateful to Rabbi Yosef Yitzchak Keller for providing me with the text originally prepared for the conclusion of the final chapter, "Reb Yitzchak the Tailor's Father." My profound thanks also to the staff and administration of Sichos In English: Rabbi Eliyahu Touger, who effected the final editorial review; Rabbi Yonah Avtzon, who managed the entire project; and Yosef Yitzchok Turner, who prepared the text for printing. I have added some explanatory footnotes and bibliographic references; these are enclosed within brackets. Footnotes without brackets appeared in the original text.

The "sitters" have been gone for a full century; *Tomchei Temimim* in Lubavitch is no more; *Tomchei Temimim* of Warsaw is gone; nearly sixty years have passed since the last issue of *HaTamim* was printed. In the interval, 770 became the central focus of *Yeshivah Tomchei Temimim*. Here, multitudes gathered, and the stories were retold. Here, new generations of chassidim were born or made, and here they were inspired. Our younger generation is rapidly assuming the role of elder chassidim, faced with the task of inspiring the coming generations. Are we up to it? Perhaps reading the biographies in this series will help. Let us study the biographies of these famous chassidic personalities; let us strive, if possible, to emulate their ways.

The last theme that the Rebbe shared with us was the imminent advent of the Messianic Age and the awakening of "those who dwell in the dust." Let us fervently pray and hope that very soon, we will meet the sitters and the *Temimim* of Lubavitch once again, together with Rashbatz and Rashdam, the Vilenker Brothers and Reb Yitzchak the Tailor, with the Rebbe and all the Rebbeim at our head, at the coming of *Moshiach*, immediately, NOW.

Shimon Neubort

Crown Heights, Brooklyn, New York
24 *Teves* 5757 [January 3, 1997]

Editor's Jottings

In 5735, for several weeks, the venerable chassid Reb Avraham Mayor would come to the *yeshivah* at Lubavitch Headquarters in 770 and *farbreng* with the students each Thursday night.

One evening, Reb Avraham focused on the difference between his days in Lubavitch and the present time: "We barely saw the Rebbe," he told the students. "He would appear in public only several times a week. Even then permission was not always granted for the *yeshivah* students to be there.

"Today, you *daven* with the Rebbe twice a day, three times a day on *Shabbos*. There are frequent *farbrengens*. It's a different world."

Reb Avraham continued to explain — without minimizing the good fortune of the present age — what had sustained him as a youth: "We had vintage Chassidim from whom we would learn. From them, we received far more than intellectual knowledge. We would watch the way they *davenned*, the way they observed *mitzvos*, the love and closeness they shared between each other. All these were lessons that we devoured."

The vintage chassidim of my student days in 770 are passing. Reb Avraham — Reb Mendel Futerfas, Reb Peretz Motchkin, Reb Nissan Nemenov and many other of the models to whom we looked up are no longer among us. I am reminded of the words of the song: "Who will be the *zaidy* if not me?"

Some might say that such thoughts are presumptuous: "Can we really expect to live up to the image of a chassid?"

Honestly, the proposition is bold. But it is the kind of boldness which is considered a positive characteristic of a "rash people."[1] We cannot afford spiritual timidity, nor is false modesty in place. We must know our limitations, but we must also know our strengths. And we must appreciate the need to employ those strengths immediately.

Mashiach is coming, and we should be prepared to greet him. And that means prepared spiritually. *Chassidus* is *Toraso shel Mashiach*, the teachings of *Mashiach*. The way we should make ourselves ready to greet *Mashiach* is by internalizing *Chassidus* and making it part of our selves.

In this endeavor, the portraits in this book are fundamentally important, for they provide us with images and examples to emulate. I don't mean that we should copy them — for the settings in which we live and the challenges of our time are different. But what was unique about these people was their capacity for spiritual renewal, that they knew how to reach into themselves and summon up spiritual strength. And that is something appropriate in all times and all places. It is a lesson which we can — and must — learn.

May this book provide us with models and enable us to become models for others.

Rarely was I ever able to sit down with several vintage chassidim together. It was difficult enough finding the opportunity to spend time with one. This book enables a reader to sit down with several Chassidim all at once. Some of the stories were written by the Previous Rebbe, others came from Chassidim. There are different tones and nuances. It's one large *farbrengen*.

---

1. *Shabbos* 88a.

May our appreciation of this *farbrengen* lead to the coming of *Mashiach* and the fulfillment of the prophecy:[2] "You who repose in the dust, arise and sing." And then we will join together with these chassidim in an actual *farbrengen;* may this take place in the immediate future.

---

2. *Yeshayahu* 26:19.

Introduction by the Editors of *HaTamim*

History of the Chassidim: Famous Personalities

B.H.

The history of the chassidim goes hand-in-hand with the history of *Toras HaChassidus*. In every generation, *Chassidus* gave rise to individuals who were unique among chassidim in devoting their whole being — heart, soul, and material resources — to *Toras HaChassidus* and the chassidic style of *avodah*. Because of this, their names are remembered with praise and renown, and have been recorded permanently by succeeding generations.

Many chassidim achieved fame even outside the circles of *Chabad Chassidus*. Others were known during their lifetimes only among their fellow chassidim, and we have had to expend much time and effort in order to gather the research material needed for a proper review of the stories of these unique personalities.

The editorial board of *HaTamim* intends to spare no effort in gathering the materials needed to produce this section on "Life Stories of Famous Personalities." We look forward to contributions of material by elder members of our society and by students of *Tomchei Temimim*. We appeal for your assistance, so that we may raise the subject of the history of the *Chabad* Chassidim to the high level it so rightfully deserves.

HaTamim, Issue No. 1, p 35a, 12-13 *Tammuz* 5695

RASHBATZ[1]

BY
ONE OF THE STUDENTS OF *TOMCHEI TEMIMIM*[2]

Rashbatz was born in the city of Szventzian, in the county of Vilna. His father spent all his time in the *beis hamedrash*, never engaging in any sort of business, while his mother headed the household and earned their livelihood. His father was a very G-d-fearing person, the descendant of a distinguished family. Though he was a *misnaged*, he heeded the prohibition against slander, and never spoke ill of the chassidic "cult." He died before the age of fifty, leaving Rashbatz an orphan.

When the mother remarried, her new husband insisted on a prenuptial stipulation concerning Rashbatz: he would only be allowed to come home for his meals, and would have to spend the rest of the day in the *beis hamedrash*; there he would also sleep.

---

1. From *HaTamim*, Issue No. 1, pp. 67-79; 12-13 *Tammuz* 5695. The editors of *HaTamim* inserted the following introductory remarks at the beginning of this article:

    > In today's first issue of *HaTamim* we present a biography of the chassid, HaRav Shmuel Betzalel, son of Reb Shalom Shabsi Sheftel, of blessed memory, known universally as "Rashbatz." This biography of Rashbatz was written by one of our fellow students of *Tomchei Temimim*, based upon what he himself heard from Rashbatz while he lived in Lubavitch.

2. [In the editorial introduction to the original article, and in the Table of Contents, the author was listed as "one of our fellow students of *Tomchei Temimim*." There is abundant evidence, however, that the actual author was none other than the Previous Rebbe himself. See Translator's Introduction.]

After some time passed, the stepfather realized that Rashbatz was a gentle lad, not likely to cause trouble; moreover, he studied with great diligence. Therefore he began to treat him more cordially, and revoked the stipulation, allowing the youth to sleep at home. He also provided him with a companion with whom he could study. In this way, nearly four years passed.

When Rashbatz reached the age of fifteen, he could already comprehend the *Gemara* and the commentary of *Tosafos* very well. He studied with diligence, spending almost all his time in the *beis hamedrash*. The leading *misnagdim*, especially Reb Hershelle (the *Rav* of Szventzian), became his close companions. The *Rav* set aside time each day to study *Gemara* and *Tosafos* with him in depth. He continued studying in this manner for over a year and a half; during this time he managed to study the three *Bavos* and the tractate *Shabbos* with the rabbi.

Nearly thirty chassidim[3] of the Alter Rebbe lived in the town of Szventzian. Once on a summer's day between *Minchah* and *Maariv* time, Rashbatz happened to pass by the *beis hamedrash* of the chassidim. Upon entering, he discovered a gathering of people sitting and studying from a small *sefer*, each perusing his own copy of the text. He felt a great desire to remain for a short while and listen to their discussion.

He approached one of the men seated there, looked into his text, and listened to the study. As he did so, one of the participants noticed that a stranger, one of their mortal enemies, was present. He began to scream at him, "What are you doing here? If you suckle the milk of the *misnagdim*, you

---

3. One of these chassidim was Reb "Itchalle the Tailor" [his story appears in a later chapter]. Rashbatz related that in this Reb Itchalle's home, chassidim would meet and review chassidic discourses while he worked at his trade.

will never become a chassid. Get out of here!" Thus, he expelled him from their midst.[4]

Being expelled upset him greatly, and as he walked he reflected on what it meant. Though he himself was a *misnaged*, he respected these chassidim in his heart. After all, he knew several of them to be Torah scholars and G-d-fearing individuals, who suffered greatly from persecution by the *misnagdim*. They also went to great expense to maintain a chassidic *shochet* who would slaughter with a finely-honed knife. The *misnagdim*, as you know, maintained a *shochet* who slaughtered with a knife that was comparatively blunt.[5]

Nevertheless, they were not intimidated by the persecutions and the excessive financial burden; on the contrary, they seemed to grow stronger all the time. This suggested to him that they were people of honor and virtue who deserved his respect. But now that they had expelled him and accused him of "suckling the milk of the *misnagdim*," he began to question their integrity. Nonetheless, he was aware that the words of the chassid who had driven him away were not simply spoken in anger; his words had been spoken deliberately, and they expressed the chassid's true sentiments.

Rashbatz was especially attracted to the chassidim by two admirable characteristics which he discerned in them. First, their great humility: they treated each other as equals. No one attempted to assume the leadership over others, and

---

4. The feud between *misnagdim* and chassidim was still in full force in those days.
5. [The Chassidim followed the ruling of the Alter Rebbe (in his *Shulchan Aruch*, Vol. VI, Responsum No. 7) to use steel knives, polished to a keen edge, for ritual slaughter. Most of the traditional Jewish communities by contrast, used iron knives, which were harder to sharpen. If they were highly polished, they would quickly become nicked, and thus, unfit for use. The nuisance of constantly resharpening and repolishing them was not considered worthwhile. In addition, the polished steel knives were considered a new innovation, which the *misnagdim* wished to avoid.]

they were always in complete agreement and harmony. Second, their attachment to the Creator: they were totally devoted to Him and to His Torah, even while they conducted business. For example, Reb Yitzchak, the tailor, would constantly repeat words of Torah as he worked. Even their merchants were constantly discussing Torah as they traded in the marketplace, and this impressed him very much.

On the other hand, he was aware of various faults in the *misnagdim*. Foremost among these was the fact that each tried to show himself to be greater than the others. They always appeared to treat one another with deference. In their hearts, however, each felt himself superior to his fellow *misnagdim*.

As Rashbatz walked along, he recalled several occasions when the *Rav*, Reb Hershelle, had revealed his haughty nature. Once, Reb Hershelle had rejected *Rashi's* commentary on a passage in *Bava Kamma*, insisting that his own understanding of the subject was superior to *Rashi's*. He would often make comments like, "*Rashi* didn't understand this *Gemara*," or "*Tosafos* missed the point!"

Rashbatz decided to investigate the chassidim and find out all their good and bad points; he would do likewise with the *misnagdim*. Then he would decide which way he preferred. Deep in his heart, he was already more attracted to the chassidim, but he was deathly afraid that their ways might not be the true path. He planned to begin his investigation by listening to the manner in which the chassidim prayed, for he had heard that *davening* was the main feature of their *avodah*.

Several days later he visited the chassidic *minyan* while they prayed. He himself was unable to *daven* with them, for the chassidim wound the *tefillin* straps (around the left arm) from right to left, while the *misnagdim* wound them from left to right.⁶ He positioned himself behind the door, confident that he would be able to hear the *davening*, for a window was open.

He stood there for more than an hour, emotionally overcome by the fervent sounds of their prayers, which were recited aloud and were accompanied by weeping. Unable to control himself, he went inside and found the *chazan* standing at the lectern and reciting, "Yours, O L-rd, is the greatness...."⁷ This was accompanied by great excitement and much weeping, while the *chazan* beat his forehead with his fists.

They all *davened* together, with great *deveikus* and devotion. At the core of his being, Rashbatz realized that they were following the proper path, and that their form of prayer was acceptable before the Holy One blessed be He. He observed that several chassidim became completely oblivious to all physical reality while *davening*, even forgetting where they were.

Their emotional involvement reached its peak during the blessings of *Kerias Shema*. On that occasion, however, he was unable to remain until the end of the prayers, for he was afraid that his Rebbe and his uncle would learn of his visit to the *beis hamedrash* of the chassidim.

From that day on a change came over him. He began to concentrate more on his prayers, and to translate the words of the prayer to himself as he *davened*. It now distressed him when he observed that several of the prominent citizens of the town — who were considered scholarly and G-d-fearing men — arrived at the *beis hamedrash* after the *davening* had

---

6. [Thus, anyone observing him while he put on the *tefillin* would immediately recognize him as a *misnaged*.]
7. [*Siddur Tehillat HaShem*, p. 37-38.]

already started. They would then begin their prayers at whatever place the congregation was up to.

This was the exact opposite of the sort of concentration that he had noticed among the chassidim during their *davening*. In addition, the *misnagdim* would not pronounce the words audibly. He therefore began to investigate the *misnagdim* in earnest, to find out exactly what they were made of.

The main subject of his inquiry was the *Rav*, Reb Hershelle, who lost no opportunity to praise his own virtues and boast of his prowess in Torah study. As he put it, he was like one of the *Rishonim*, who had no use at all for the commentaries of the *Acharonim*. He was able to find everything in the original Talmudic text;[8] he could swim across the "River of the *Rambam*" with a single stroke, while *Piskei HaRosh* and *Tosafos* were like his own two eyes.

He would often say of himself, "I — Reb Hirsh — use the *Talmud* and *Tosafos* for a pillow under my head, and the *Yerushalmi*, *Sifra*, and the *Rambam* for cushions under my sides. Is it for nothing that for thirty years (thank G-d), I have studied with great diligence, more than eighteen hours a day?"

Reb Hirsh made it a point to get the *davening* over as quickly as possible. His prayers never took more than a half hour, even on *Yom Tov*. When the *davening* was over, his face would take on an expression of delight, as though he had rid himself of a heavy burden. Nevertheless, Rashbatz' studied with Reb Hirsh ever more persistently, for he had a great craving to study; diligent Torah study was his one and only desire.

The *Rav*, for his part, found Rashbatz to be an apt pupil. He therefore became even more friendly to him, devoting to

---

8. [With no need for any commentaries.]

him many hours of the day. He took great delight in studying with the lad in depth, all day long and part of the night.

Rashbatz' visit to the chassidic *minyan* produced one permanent result: he was now more concerned with his *davening*. Though there was not much he could do about it openly, deep in his heart he harbored a great desire to pray with more concentration. As time went on, he became repelled by the *misnagdim* because of the rapid pace of their *davening*, and the way they always boasted about themselves.

One day, as he studied a certain *Aggadah* with Reb Hirsh, the conversation turned to the topic of prayer. He then asked the *Rav*, "What is the meaning of praying with concentration?"

"That's not for us!" replied the *Rav*. "Only the greatest among Israel are capable of that."

To this Rashbatz remarked, "But you, my Rebbe, are a giant and a prince among Jews. And so, why don't *you* spend more time *davening*? Why do you hurry through it so?"

"When it comes to Torah study," said Reb Hirsh, "I am (thank G-d) one of the greats among Israel, unique in this generation. But I have nothing to do with the things you mentioned. Only members of 'the cult' [*daven* at length. But they] are all liars and charlatans, engaging in their strange practices. May G-d save us from them!"

Hearing this answer, Rashbatz became very upset. He then inquired whether the *Rav* had ever spoken or debated with members of the cult. Had he investigated them at all, to find out whether what people said about them was true? Or had he simply made up his mind about them without looking into the facts? Were his opinions based upon hatred passed on from one person to the next? Did he also harbor this hatred without bothering to find out what the chassidim were? If he did pursue a rational investigation, perhaps he might discover that the rumors he had heard were untrue. Or [even if true], perhaps the chassidim had since changed their ways.

When he heard these arguments, the *Rav* had no idea that they were the result of carefully-planned research into the subject. He ascribed it to the fact that the lad — though highly gifted — was young and inexperienced, and unaware of the wicked deeds of the chassidim. Since no one had ever explained to him exactly what chassidim were, or what their aims were, his questions stemmed from simple innocence.

Nevertheless, the *Rav* was pleased to discover that Rashbatz possessed such acute mental abilities. He resolved to take upon himself the holy task of educating the boy in the secrets of the chassidim, their philosophy, and their early history. He began repeating to him — a little at a time — disparaging stories about the chassidim and their great Rebbe (the Alter Rebbe), which he had heard "from eminent people."

These stories continued over many days. On one occasion the *Rav* boasted that he had eaten lunch with an informant who had betrayed the Alter Rebbe [to the government]. Rashbatz begged him to relate the whole story of how this denunciation had taken place. Reb Hirsh told him everything he knew about the affair. Whenever he mentioned one of the informants by name, he added an honorific title such as *"gaon," "tzaddik,"* and the like. Rashbatz then asked, "Isn't it forbidden to hand a Jew over to gentile authorities?[9] And if so, why do you honor such people with the titles *tzaddik* and *gaon*?"

---

9. [See *Rambam, Mishneh Torah, Hilchos Choveil U'Mazik*, ch. 8.]

Reb Hirsh replied that one of the foremost disciples of the *Gaon* Rabbi Eliyahu of Vilna had ruled that it was permitted by law. He then began to praise the Vilna *Gaon* and his disciples with superlatives, all however materially [rather than spiritually] oriented. The lesson to be learned from all of this, he told Rashbatz, was that he must not even look at the chassidim. Even more so, he must never visit their congregation (G-d forbid), for their ways bordered on apostasy and heresy (may G-d preserve us). He warned him against this in the strongest terms.

This conversation was a revelation to Rashbatz. Most of what the *misnagdim* said against the chassidim stemmed from secret hatred and jealousy, passed on from one person to the next, unsupported by any real evidence. On the contrary, it appeared to him that the chassidim could easily prove their innocence. They had committed no sin, for they were following the path of holiness. He decided to visit them while they studied between *Minchah* and *Maariv*. He would find out just what they were studying, and what this subject matter was all about. After seeing all this, he would be able to decide for himself which path to follow.

The day arrived when he resolved to carry out his plan, and visit the chassidic *minyan* to see what sort of subject matter they were studying. He decided to take precautions to avoid being expelled as on the previous occasion. The best way to do this, [he thought,] was to confide in one of the chassidim and tell him everything: since he now knew a little about the chassidim and their ways, he desired to visit their congregation, for in his heart he was attracted to them.

Just before sunset, he approached one of the chassidim and told him the story. He begged him to give him protection so that he would not be expelled. This chassid was very friendly to him, and advised him not to come during the study session. Instead, he himself would set aside some time to teach him what the subject was about, what *Chassidus* was based on, and what the origins of the chassidim were. Then he would know what to do, and could make whatever decision he chose. Rashbatz agreed to this plan.

This chassid, who was an employee of Reb Yitzchak the Tailor, met with Rashbatz each evening at a designated place. He told him that there had once lived a great and exalted person called the Baal Shem Tov. He described several of the Baal Shem Tov's wonders and miracles, adding that initially everything had been carried out in total secrecy. Then he described how the Baal Shem Tov had gradually revealed himself. He told him about the Baal Shem Tov's disciples, and that after his passing he was succeeded by our great Rebbe, the *Maggid* of Mezritch, followed by his eminent disciple Reb Menachem Mendel of Vitebsk. Later, Reb Mendel departed for the Holy Land, and he was succeeded by the Alter Rebbe.

He described the feud and the denunciation of the Alter Rebbe, and the miracles by which he had been saved. Over a period of several days, he enlightened Rashbatz and informed him of the entire history. Through these stories, he demonstrated to him the greatness and holiness of the Alter Rebbe's personality, the essential features of the teachings of *Chassidus*, and the *avodah* of the heart which constitutes the chassidic way of life.

Among the original *misnagdim*, [the chassid explained,] there were many personalities of importance; alas, they fell into the trap of "harboring suspicions against the innocent." The *misnagdim* of later generations merely followed in the footsteps of their predecessors, and none of them knew for certain exactly what the chassidim were or what they stood for.

Rashbatz was very attracted by the stories he heard from the chassid, and his desire to join the chassidim and to follow their ways grew ever stronger. He told the chassid that he wished to investigate the study of *Chassidus* further. The chassid complied, and took him along to the next few study sessions. He allowed Rashbatz to sit next to him, and he explained to him each topic that was being studied.

Among the *misnagdim*, no one was aware of these visits. Once, while they were studying *Tanya*, Rashbatz found the subject quite difficult, for he was still a young lad. The chassid advised him to take a copy of the text with him and review the lesson at his leisure. This suggestion made good sense to him, and that is what he did. He went to his own *beis hamedrash*, and sat down to review the lesson once or twice; this became a regular habit with him.

One night, as he sat alone in the *beis hamedrash* and reviewed his studies, a *misnaged* entered. He was quite gratified to see a young fellow studying with such great diligence and intensity. Approaching the lad, he noticed the small volume in which he was engrossed; he sat down nearby to listen, and was pleased with what he heard. Rashbatz was completely unaware that anyone had entered, and he continued studying.

Eventually he raised his eyes. Discovering the man seated opposite him, he grew very frightened. In confusion and terror he cried out, "*Oy! Oy!*" (for now his secret was discovered, and an unpleasant future awaited him). He seized the text and hastily thrust it into his pocket.

His confusion aroused the man's suspicions and prompted him to inquire about the subject he had been studying, saying that it had sounded like a very interesting topic. Rashbatz, however, suspected that the man was humoring him so that he would not deny what he had really been studying.

The longer the man continued to praise what he had heard, the more reluctant Rashbatz became to discuss it. Since he refused to reply, the man suddenly overpowered him and confiscated the text. He examined it, but had no idea what it was until he came upon the words "*tzaddik, rasha, beinoni.*" Now he knew that it was the handbook of the chassidic cult. That was why Rashbatz had become so frightened and confused, refusing to show him the text.

The man went to Reb Hershelle and reported to him that early in the morning, at three or four o'clock (it was summertime), he had discovered the boy in the *beis hamedrash* intently studying a textbook of the cult.

"I arrived at the *beis hamedrash* before sunrise and discovered this lad studying with great diligence and depth. I caught only a few isolated phrases:

> Even regarding interpersonal relations, he should suppress every sort of bias, anger, and grudge; not only does he accept suffering at the hands of his fellow Jew, but he even rewards him for it.[10]

"I was overjoyed to hear this young fellow studying so early in the morning, and with such diligence. But when he noticed me, he became very agitated and began to scream. He then grabbed the *sefer* and hid it in his pocket. It was then that I realized he must have been subverted by heresy, and was studying a *sefer* of the cult. Calling upon the Name of the Holy One (blessed be He), I gathered all my strength and wrestled with him until I managed to take the *sefer* from him. Here it is!"

---

10. Rashbatz was then reviewing *Tanya*, Chapter 12.

"The Creator has bestowed a great privilege upon you," said Reb Hirsh. "You have managed to save a Jewish soul. As for the *sefer*, we must show it to his uncle. Let him see for himself what sort of upbringing the boy has received in his house. Since you began the *mitzvah*, you may have the privilege of finishing it.[11] Go at once and tell his uncle to come to me!"

When the uncle was brought before Reb Hirsh, the man related to him all that he had seen with his own eyes, and showed him the textbook of the cult that he had found in his possession. Reb Hirsh warned the uncle that studying such subject matter can easily lead to heresy (G-d forbid).

Rashbatz, meanwhile, was afraid to remain in the *beis hamedrash*; at first he had planned to attend the chassidic *minyan*, but he was afraid to do that too. Finally, he concealed himself on the roof of the *beis hamedrash*, where there was a skylight through which he could hear everything that happened below. When he saw that the sunrise *minyan* had finished and departed, he went downstairs and entered the *beis hamedrash* to *daven*. He was greatly relieved that no one had spoken of the affair, and he decided that it would be best if things remained so.

After *davening*, he went to his mother's house for breakfast, as he did every morning. But as he entered the house, while still crossing the threshold, his uncle struck him a severe blow to the head with a length of wooden board. Without saying a word, he proceeded to beat him with his fists until the lad fainted from the pain. Seeing him faint, his mother began to cry out bitterly; her screams restored Rashbatz to consciousness.

The uncle began to yell at her, "Should I keep an *apikores* in my house? You'd be better off if he were dead! I would

---

11. [See *Tanchuma, Eikev*, sec. 6; *Rashi, Devarim* 8:1.]

have left him unconscious until he died. You're only a woman, so you take pity on him. But remember: if he survives and becomes an *apikores*, you'll wish he had died now, while he's still a religious Jew."

A few days later, when Rashbatz had recovered from the beating, he went to the *beis hamedrash* as he had always done. But instead of studying with him, the *Rav* began to admonish him for his terrible sin. He told him that he had fallen into a trap and been brainwashed by "them." He went on and on in this vein, but Rashbatz remained silent, offering no reply. Then the *Rav* began to badger him about doing *teshuvah*:

"Will you commit such foolishness again, or will you take pity on your own soul and promise never again to visit their congregation?"

To this too, Rashbatz made no reply. Instead, he began to refute the *Rav's* arguments, insisting that the chassidic way was the true way, and it was the *misnagdim* who were wrong. "When they realize they are mistaken, they too will mend their ways."

The *Rav* saw that Rashbatz knew more about the history and the events of the controversy than he did, and he therefore despaired of inspiring him to do *teshuvah*. He notified the uncle that it was a lost cause, and that the lad had fallen into a trap from which there was no escape. When the uncle heard this, he swore that he would evict Rashbatz from his house; he would not allow him to remain another minute.

The *Rav* cautioned all his congregants that the boy had been subverted by the cult, and they must be wary of him. After this, they all subjected him to a great deal of abuse, hoping that this would prompt him to repent.

Since his uncle had thrown him out of the house, he went to the *beis hamedrash*. Though the congregants didn't expel him, each chastised him, calling him *"apikores"* and other names. He was forced to go hungry on the first day. Then, over the next three or four days he remained inadequately fed, for his mother brought him only some dry bread to still his hunger. This situation continued through *Shabbos*.

On *Shabbos* after *davening*, he went for a walk beyond the city limits, where he began to cry. "Master of the Universe! I wish only to follow the true path of holiness. If the path of the *misnagdim* is the true one, I will follow it unswervingly; if the path of the chassidim is the true one, I will join their congregation and follow in their ways." He then wept bitter tears.

When he returned to town he set a sign for himself: if the first person he met was a chassid, he would join the chassidim; if he was a *misnaged*, he would join the *misnagdim*. He resolved to obey this sign, and implored G-d — the Father of orphans — to take pity upon him and show him the correct path. As he entered the town and walked along the first street, he met no one. Most of the common folk were asleep, while the Torah scholars were busy studying, either at home or in the *batei hamedrash*.

Continuing a bit farther, he saw Reb Hershelle walking with two other people. This sight saddened him, for deep in his heart he had been certain that he would be joining the chassidim. Now, however, he spied Reb Hershelle walking in the distance. But wait a minute — there was still hope! He was still some distance away, and he might yet meet a chassid first. As he walked further, he rejoiced to see several chassidim emerging from their *beis hamedrash*; unfortunately, they turned the other way and disappeared, without his meeting them.

A moment later, to Rashbatz' great relief, two men emerged from the chassidic *beis hamedrash*; one of them was the chassid he had originally approached. He was very happy to see them, especially since they were walking toward him, and their gestures indicated that they were talking about him. One of the chassidim pointed him out to the other.

The whole town was already repeating the story of the lad to whom the *Rav* had devoted so much energy, and who had studied with such diligence and aptitude, but had later fallen into the hands of the cult. He had been caught studying one of their textbooks, and his uncle had beaten him and driven him from his home. Within a few minutes the chassidim reached him and he wished them "Good *Shabbos!*"

"What shall we do with you?" asked the first chassid, "you're a lost cause. If you deny what has happened to you, you will remain a *misnaged*. It seems that you don't deserve to become a chassid. Woe to you in that case! Even if all the wisdom in the world enters your head, you will never be any better than you are now."

In reply, Rashbatz related all that had happened to him since the day the man had discovered him studying. He described all his suffering, and told of the sign he had set for himself. Now, he was ready to become a member of their society, and to do whatever they required of him. The chassid took him to his home and gave him food and drink, though he himself was quite poor.

The following Monday the *Rav* and the uncle discovered that Rashbatz had remained with the chassidim. The uncle began to torment the lad's mother, causing her much pain and anguish. Being a clever woman, she sent for her son to hear his side of the story. He explained it all to her, and she was forced to admit that he had chosen the correct path and should continue to follow it.

The chassid studied *Chassidus* with him daily; at first they studied *Tanya*, reviewing each chapter four or five times. They also studied *Shaarei Orah* by the Mitteler Rebbe, which Rashbatz studied with diligence and great relish. Each subject he studied was reviewed several times; there were occasions when he would review the same passage twenty or thirty times.

During one of his *farbrengens* [after he became a *mashpia*] Rashbatz admonished the students of *Tomchei Temimim*: "When I was a young lad, if we heard a teaching from the elder chassidim we would kiss the soles of their feet. On the other hand, you young fellows are spoon-fed like fattened calves, but you pay no attention. I used to sit for five or six hours reviewing a single passage that the chassid Reb Moshe had taught me.

"This Reb Moshe advised me that after thoroughly reviewing the lesson verbally, I should review it three or four times in my mind. Thus, I accustomed myself to concentrate on a single thought for more than three hours.

"[The manner in which the chassidim studied *Nigleh*, the revealed teachings of Torah law, was also unique.] Had I not seen it with my own eyes and heard it with my own ears, I would never have believed that chassidim could study *Gemara* in such depth, or that they were capable of developing such logical and novel insights. Three times a week, the chassidim held in-depth study sessions of *Talmud*. I was in for quite a surprise when I attended my first such session.

"I then learned that the Alter Rebbe had instructed each congregation and community of chassidim to study the entire *Talmud* every year. For this purpose, each individual would choose one tractate to study by himself. In this way, they could collectively complete the entire *Talmud*. In addition, they chose one tractate which all studied together in depth; this study session was held only three times a week. Each time I attended this lecture I learned something new. My study of Chapter 5 in the *Tanya* created a great desire within me to study Torah even more intensely than before."

One day Rashbatz happened to meet Reb Hirsh, and he greeted his former teacher with *Shalom Aleichem!* At first Reb Hirsh turned away without answering, but a moment later he called Rashbatz by name and inquired whether he had repented his wicked ways. Rashbatz changed the subject, posing a serious question concerning the Talmudic subject he was then studying that had disturbed him.

Reb Hirsh pondered deeply into the question and then proceeded to explain the entire topic with a deep and complex *pilpul*, during which he refuted *Rashi's* commentary. Rashbatz responded by reciting his own understanding of the topic. Reb Hirsh was amazed, declaring that this was an excellent approach to the subject, and that the lad had apparently made much progress in *Talmud* since they had last met.

Rashbatz then began to explain to Reb Hirsh and the other dignitaries of the *beis hamedrash* what the essential features of the teachings of *Chassidus* were: the *mitzvos* of believing in G-d, declaring His Oneness, loving Him, and fearing Him. Without a knowledge of the teachings of *Chassidus*, it is impossible to fulfill these *mitzvos* properly. Even ordinary Torah study, and the *mitzvos* governing interpersonal relationships, are on a far higher plane when understood in the light of *Chassidus*.

Suddenly, right in the middle of his speech, one of the young *misnagdim* struck him such a powerful blow to the cheek that his head snapped from left to right and back again, and his whole body reverberated. His hat flew off his head, but before he could pick it up blood began to pour from his mouth and nose, and he fell unconscious. When he came to, he discovered that he was lying on the floor in the *shul* where the chassidim prayed. They then told him what had happened.

After he had fainted, the *misnagdim* had continued to beat him mercilessly. Some of them suggested that he should be beaten to death, but Reb Hirsh and a few other prominent scholars had opposed this. Being no match for the assailants, they sent for the chassidim, all of whom immediately came. With the help of Reb Hirsh and the prominent scholars, they managed to rescue him and carry him to the chassidic *shul*.

They worked very hard to bring him out of his coma, but he remained lying there inert as a stone, burning with fever, his eyes shut, and his mouth open. The doctor declared that he was suffering from both swelling of the brain and pneumonia. He administered various medicines and tried different procedures, but it was three weeks before the patient finally opened his eyes and gradually began to recognize people.

For a long time he had no idea how he had become sick. He had no memory at all of his meeting with Reb Hirsh, his learned discussion, his speech about *Chassidus*, or the beating he had received. After he recovered fully, the chassidim would not let him go outside by himself, for they were afraid that the *misnagdim* would beat him again. He therefore spent his days studying in the home of the chassid Reb Moshe, and would go to the *beis hamedrash* only in his company. Thus, he continued to study the revealed aspects of Torah as well as *Chassidus* until the middle of the month of Shvat.

The time he spent living among the chassidim — from midsummer until Shvat — passed very quickly, for it was a period of joy and delight to his soul. Each individual chassid made a strong effort to befriend him and demonstrate to him that the ways of the chassidim represented the true path. He absorbed everything he was taught, for to him the words of the chassidim were fragrant oil and life-giving dew. He was particularly impressed by their complete dedication and devotion to instructing him in the true path of the teachings of *Chassidus*.

During this time, the chassidim came to appreciate his superior intellectual abilities and his unique powers of concentration. The more astute among them predicted that the lad would have a glorious future in the study of *Chassidus*. He was also remarkably persevering, never retreating from pursuing any goal he set for himself, even in the face of great obstacles and impediments. He followed whatever path he chose, with complete self-assurance, acting as if there were no objection, and as if all were in agreement with his choice.

The chassidim advised him that he could proceed further in achieving his goal if he traveled to one of the renowned chassidim and became his apprentice. After he spent some time there, he would be qualified to travel to Lubavitch, where the Rebbe the *Tzemach Tzedek* lived.

One day the chassidim held a convention in Szventzian to explore ways of improving the situation of chassidim and *Chassidus* in their vicinity. One of the topics on the agenda was finding a proper place for their developing student — Rashbatz — to study.

After carefully considering several suggestions, they decided to send him to Reb Michel Opotzker, who had been one of the foremost chassidim of the Alter Rebbe, and who was known to possess *ruach hakodesh*. Under his guidance, the lad would achieve his goal in studying *Chassidus* and would become accustomed to *davening*, which constitutes "*avodah* of the heart." This chassid, Reb Michel Opotzker, would teach him and prepare him for his eventual trip to Lubavitch.

One day, the chassid Reb Moshe told Rashbatz that — at their recent convention — the chassidim had discussed his current situation, and what they thought he was capable of achieving in the end. They had concluded that it would be best for him to travel to Lubavitch, where he would attend the senior *yeshivah*. In Lubavitch he could continue to study *Chassidus* and he would hear chassidic discourses from the Rebbe.

However, in order to gain admission to the Lubavitcher *Yeshivah*, one needed advance preparation in both studying and *davening*, under the tutelage of a chassid who was well known for both his scholarship and his *avodah*. They had therefore chosen to send him to Reb Michel Opotzker. If he agreed, they would take the necessary steps to put this plan into action.

Of course, Rashbatz consented to the plan. Although he did not understand the suggestion totally, he was sure that they had his best interests at heart.

Sometime during the month of Adar, one of the chassidim had occasion to travel to Lubavitch. He offered to take Rashbatz with him, for the route they traveled in those days passed by the city where Reb Michel lived. He would deliver the lad to Reb Michel as they had agreed, and request that Reb Michel accept him and teach him whatever he needed to know about the teachings of *Chassidus*. He would also ask Reb Michel to keep an eye on him during his training, so that he would follow the correct path and eventually become a full-fledged chassid, and a proper "vessel" to absorb the teachings of *Chassidus*.

This would constitute payment for the suffering and persecution the chassidim had experienced at the hands of the *misnagdim* on his account. The chassidim readily agreed to this, for it was obviously preferable to send him with one of their brethren than to let him go by himself.

Those days were a period of inner turmoil for Rashbatz. At first he planned to depart at once with the chassid, without bidding farewell to the *misnagdim* who were his former friends and acquaintances. Although he was very warm and loved truth and strict etiquette, he was reluctant to visit the *misnagdim*. When he compared them to the chassidim, and recalled the suffering and persecution they had subjected them to, he could not bear to have anything to do with them.

"It is the forbearing nature of the chassidim that allowed all this to occur," thought Rashbatz. Possibly even they would be unable to endure it in silence, were it not for the oft-repeated warning of the Alter Rebbe to the chassidic communities (printed in *Iggeres HaKodesh*, Epistle 2, beginning with the words "I have become small..."). Because of this warning, the chassidim feared even to engage the *misnagdim* in conversation, and they unanimously resolved to accept whatever happened to them, without protest.

Upon reflection, however, he decided that he would do the reverse, and take leave of his former companions. After all, he was about to depart for an indefinite period; who knew when he would ever see them again? He owed them thanks for all the kindness they had shown him before he joined the chassidim. When would he have another chance to express it? He did not tell even his teacher Reb Moshe about his decision to bid farewell to the *misnagdim*, for he was afraid they would not let him go.

Actually, he was also a bit afraid that the *misnagdim* would beat him as they had already done before. But his sincere desire to see them again spurred his decision to go and say goodbye to them, especially to Reb Hirsh. He and a few of the Torah scholars had opposed the beating, and had even sent for the chassidim to come quickly and rescue him; in fact, they themselves had assisted in saving him. Therefore, he would visit Reb Hirsh first.

At an opportune time, Rashbatz went to Reb Hirsh and found him sitting with two others, discussing a *pilpul* on a certain Torah subject. Fortuitously, Rashbatz had only recently made a thorough study of that same topic, and he thus had a ready excuse for joining their conversation. At first the *Rav* reacted toward him as though he were a former Torah student who had gone astray, but it was nevertheless evident that he still loved him in his heart.

Within a few moments Rashbatz had joined the discussion circle, and his logical arguments gratified the *Rav* who now turned to him and inquired into his spiritual well-being. After a brief conversation he satisfied himself that the fears he had entertained when Rashbatz had joined the chassidim had been groundless.

When the other scholars departed, and Reb Hirsh and Rashbatz remained alone, they began to debate the subject of *misnagdim* vs. chassidim. Rashbatz recited a long list of deeds and attributes in which the chassidim were superior, along with a list of the *misnagdim's* shortcomings. He demonstrated to Reb Hirsh that in most cases the chassidim were right, and that the *misnagdim* had gained the upper hand only because of the great devotion of the chassidim to the Alter Rebbe. Otherwise, the chassidim would have long ago proved they were the real *tzaddikim*, and that they deserved credit for their great forbearance and humility.

Reb Hirsh was forced to admit that Rashbatz was right about several of his main points. In addition, he had no reply or excuse for many of the questions Rashbatz posed concerning the behavior and customs of the *misnagdim*.

This conversation greatly elevated Rashbatz in Reb Hirsh's estimation, and he began to inquire further into his spiritual status. Rashbatz then told him of the decision of his chassidic mentors to send him to one of the prominent chassidim, with whom he would study for a while, until he became worthy of making the trip to Lubavitch. The reason he had come here now was to bid him farewell for an indefinite period.

When Reb Hirsh heard this, he became very upset and declared that — in spite of the fact that he had heard the Lubavitcher Rebbe was a great *gaon* — in his opinion Rashbatz would be better off remaining at home and studying with him. He tried to convince him to remain in Szventzian and continue to study the revealed aspects of Torah for at least two or three years — then he could go where he wished.

Rashbatz replied that his chassidic teachers feared that without studying the chassidic approach to Torah, he might forget who the Giver of the Torah was, and therefore they had decided he must leave. The chassid to whom they were sending him would set him on the right path. When he finished speaking, they began saying their goodbyes. The *Rav's* eyes almost overflowed with tears as he begged the lad at least to remain a Torah-observant Jew.

Rashbatz was quite moved by these last remarks. They proved that the chassidim were correct when they said that the *misnagdim* still held on to the foolish notion that the study of *Chassidus* detracts from studying the revealed aspects of Torah. Any sensible person could see that just the opposite was true: *Chassidus* only enhances the Torah, as evidenced by many instances where chassidim were more scrupulous in their religious observance than the *misnagdim*. As the Alter Rebbe explains, it was the measure of *chumtin* [sandy soil, containing certain mineral substances which preserves many more measures of grain].[12] With these emotions, he took his leave.

A few days later, the time arrived for him to depart with the chassid. The chassidim assembled to wish him a successful journey. He departed in the chassid's company, with both joy and sadness in his heart. Once they were on their way, Rashbatz began to beg the chassid to take him along to Lubavitch, for he greatly desired to see the holy Rebbe. However, the chassid refused, saying that he had no authority to undertake such a thing without permission from the whole chassidic congregation. Moreover, he himself also felt that he ought to take him first to Reb Michel; only after he spent some time there would he be worthy of traveling to Lubavitch.

Rashbatz then begged to be allowed to make at least a short visit to Lubavitch — only for as long as the chassid remained there — then he would go with him [to Reb Michel] on the return trip. The chassid explained that it would be much better for him to go straight there. Eventually Rashbatz agreed, and three days before Purim they arrived at Reb Michel's home.

Upon their arrival Reb Michel wished them both *Shalom Aleichem!* and exclaimed, "Is this one of the 'souls that you have acquired'[13] in Szventzian? Fine! Very good!" He greeted Rashbatz warmly and began to explain to him what *Chassidus* was all about. He told him that it is an exceedingly

---

12. [Rashbatz was alluding to *Likkutei Torah, Parshas Vayikra*. There, as an analogy, the Alter Rebbe cites *Shabbos* 31b which states that to preserve 24 measures of grain, one should mix in one measure of *chumtin*. The revealed dimensions of Torah law can be compared to the grain, which is preserved by the study of *Chassidus*.]
13. [I.e., one of the people whom you have attracted to *Chassidus*; cf. *Bereishis* 12:5.]

difficult system of *avodah*, and one needs the assistance of Heaven to follow it successfully.

The main feature of this *avodah* is that everything must be done with truth, without deceiving oneself. He taught Rashbatz about the new approach to the Baal Shem Tov's teachings that the Alter Rebbe had initiated. In general, he addressed him in the way one would speak to a prospective convert to Judaism.

Reb Michel's customs were unique; he spent all his time studying and *davening* in the attic, admitting no one except his new apprentice. He *davened* with intense fervor, and spent all day and night in constant study. He never traveled to Lubavitch, but he had once visited the Alter Rebbe, author of the *Tanya*, in Liozna. He had spent four years there, and after that he had never visited any other Rebbe.

A favorite expression of his was: "I am unable to rise to their level, and they are unable to limit their radiance [to my level]. The Alter Rebbe, on the other hand, knew how to reveal his splendor, but at the same time he could also limit its intensity."

Whenever a chassid passed through Reb Michel's town on his way to Lubavitch, Reb Michel would carry his baggage for him and accompany him for two of three miles. Other than that, he never left his hometown. Though he was a great Torah scholar, he refused to accept a position as a *Rav*, for he despised the very idea of it. He avoided conversation with other people as much as possible, preferring to remain in seclusion.

Rashbatz remained there for a year and a half, constantly studying Torah and *Chassidus* under Reb Michel's guidance. "Under Reb Michel, I acquired the fundamental principles of *Chassidus* and the ability to conceive of abstract concepts which *Chassidus* teaches," Rashbatz related. "There, I clearly perceived the Divine radiance. Reb Michel would often say, 'This is what I heard from our Great Rebbe.' I was constantly overjoyed at my good fortune in being a student of Reb Michel."

One day, Reb Michel Opotzker informed Rashbatz that he no longer wished to have him as a pupil, and advised him to travel to Lubavitch. He explained that Rashbatz had already achieved the purpose for which he had come, and there was nothing more to be gained by remaining with him.

Hearing this, Rashbatz' eyes filled with tears of joy. He immediately agreed to follow this advice, on condition that Reb Michel grant him one request: to teach him what he should ask the Rebbe for. The chassid Reb Michel answered all his questions, and also taught him what he should request of the Rebbe (Rashbatz never revealed what Reb Michel told him in this regard).

Rashbatz remained with Reb Michel during the High Holy Days, and after Sukkos he began to prepare for his trip. He had come from Szventzian to Opotzk on foot, and on foot he traveled from Opotzk to Lubavitch. He arrived in Lubavitch on Friday of *Parshas Mishpatim*, the first day of *Rosh Chodesh* Adar I, 5608 [February 4, 1848], thus attaining his heart's desire, for which he had waited so long.

Upon his departure, Reb Michel gave him a letter of reference addressed to the Rebbe the *Tzemach Tzedek*, cautioning him not to read it. It goes without saying that [at the outset], out of respect (and even more, out of fear) he did not dare to read the note. Eventually, however, his curiosity got the best of him; he unfolded the sheet of paper, but to his great amazement it was totally blank; not a single word was written on it!

Thursday, *Erev Rosh Chodesh* Adar I, he left the town of Dobramisl, and on the same day he managed to reach the inn in Berezovne, about seven miles from Lubavitch. The innkeeper served him supper, and at six o'clock in the evening he lay down to rest. The innkeeper woke him at about one in the morning, for one of the butchers was going to Lubavitch, and Rashbatz was to go with him.

When he arrived in Lubavitch it was still several hours before daybreak; he entered the Rebbe's *shul* and positioned himself near the stove. Upon entering the *shul* he found a few of the young men sitting and studying. They greeted him with *Shalom Aleichem!* and inquired where he came from, but he made no reply. Sitting next to the stove, he soon fell asleep.

He awoke suddenly, to the sound of someone loudly calling out the name of Reb Michel Opotzker. One of the elder chassidim was crying "Where is the fellow who came here with a note from the chassid Reb Michel Opotzker?"

Approaching the elder man, Rashbatz said, "It is I who brought the note from Reb Michel Opotzker."

"Why didn't you answer me the first time," rebuked the vintage chassid, "I've had to call you three times without a reply. Follow me! The Rebbe has summoned you to his chamber."

With fear and apprehension he entered the Rebbe's room, all his limbs trembling. The Rebbe reprimanded him severely for disobeying Reb Michel's instructions and reading the note he had given him.

Whenever Rashbatz recalled the words spoken to him by the *Tzemach Tzedek* on that occasion, he would break into bitter weeping and say, "Someone who was born a *misnaged* must undergo a special kind of refinement [in order to become a chassid]."

He was about nineteen years old when he arrived in Lubavitch, and it was then that he began to feel an irresistible urge to study the revealed aspects of Torah. He would frequently describe this overwhelming desire to study Torah which he experienced on the first day of his arrival in Lubavitch, as a "burning fire." Though he was thoroughly exhausted from his long trip, and he felt his whole body falling apart, he could not restrain himself: he took a *Gemara*, and sat down to study all day.

What pleasure and bliss he felt on that first day! He recalled all his past aspirations, which were now fulfilled. He had now achieved the purpose for which he had abandoned his birthplace and his family, including his own mother who was dearer to him than anything in the world. Reflecting on this, his eyes filled with tears. But he made a firm commitment, then and there, to dedicate his life and his fortune to the Rebbe the *Tzemach Tzedek*. He would forget his family and even his own mother, for the Rebbe would now be his father. He would view this day as the day of his birth, and Lubavitch would be his new family.

The day passed and evening came. After *Kabbalas Shabbos*, many chassidim began to assemble in the *minyan* room. There was a great deal of crowding and jostling, and Rashbatz himself found himself crushed against the wall. When he inquired what was happening now, they told him that this was the appointed time for the Torah discourse, and the Rebbe would arrive shortly to deliver his public address.

After about half an hour, several imposing men entered and took their places next to the platform, which stood in the center of the *beis hamedrash*. They were the Rebbe's sons, and they were dressed in silk, and wore round sable fur hats on their heads. They were accompanied by a few dignitaries, who went up onto the platform. The entire audience then began elbowing their way closer to the platform, for the *beis hamedrash* was filled wall-to-wall with people.

In the midst of the tumult, silence suddenly prevailed and the crowd parted, leaving a wide path in the middle. The Rebbe entered, wearing white silk garments and a white *shtreimel* on his head. Ascending the platform and sitting in his place, he began to speak about the verse,[14] "If you lend silver to My people...." [The *Tzemach Tzedek* explained]:

> "Silver" refers to the soul, which constantly desires and aspires to ascend upwards,[15] as is written,[16] "The spirit of *Adam* (man) constantly ascends."
>
> "*Adam*" refers to the souls of the Jewish people, as is written,[17] "You are *Adam*." Our sages explain[18] that "You," [i.e., the Jews exclusively] are called *Adam*. The soul is given to man as a loan, as is written,[19] "The days are parceled out," i.e., [each person is granted] a finite number [of days]. If one squanders a day, he forfeits one of his [spiritual] garments.

This teaching made a mighty impression on Rashbatz and it excited his spirit, for he was already well versed in *Chassidus*. When the Rebbe finished his lecture, he departed, and his sons also went home. Rashbatz went to look for a place to stay, and one of the residents of the town, Reb David Czerkes, invited him to eat at his home that *Shabbos*, and gave him a place to sleep.

After *Shabbos*, he desired to enter the Rebbe's room for a private audience. He presented this request to the butler,

---

14. [*Shmos* 22:14.]
15. [A play on words: the Hebrew word for "silver" (כסף) has the same root as the word for "desire".]
16. [*Koheles* 3:21.]
17. [*Yechezkel* 34:31.]
18. [*Yevamos* 61a explains that "you" refers to the Jewish people. They are called "Adam," and no other nation is called "Adam."]
19. [*Tehillim* 139:16. We have translated the verse as appropriate to the context of this teaching. Within the chapter of *Tehillim*, other translations are suggested.]

Reb Chayim Dov, who flatly refused him. A few days later, however, Reb [Yehudah] Leib,[20] one of the Rebbe's sons, became acquainted with him and promised to try and get him admitted on the following week, which he did.

Rashbatz never revealed what the Rebbe told him in private (unlike many other famous chassidim, who disclosed details of their *yechidus*). All he would say was that the Rebbe had told him "You know how to study, so you may study in my *yeshivah* together with the local young men."

To this, he had replied, "But Rebbe, I came here to learn how to *daven!*"[21]

The next day the custodian informed him that he had been allocated an allowance of forty pennies a week, which he would deliver to him. After that, he remained there to study Torah and *daven*. He became a close friend of all the Rebbe's sons.

For two years Rashbatz studied Torah and *Chassidus* undisturbed. The Rebbe's son Reb Yehudah Leib suggested to him a match with the daughter of one of the residents of Lubavitch, to which he agreed. The wedding took place in the year 5610 [1850], and his father-in-law undertook to support him for several years.

Rashbatz often said, "I spent seven rich years in Lubavitch, the seven years from 5608 to 5615 [1848-1855], constantly studying the revealed Torah and *Chassidus*. Thank G-d, I came into the good graces of the Rebbe's youngest son Reb Shmuel, the Rebbe Maharash. He would review with me

---

20. [He later became the Rebbe of Kapust.]
21. [According to tradition, when the Alter Rebbe set out from home he had not yet made up his mind whether to travel to Vilna or to Mezritch. He had heard that in Vilna they taught one how to study, but in Mezritch they taught one how to *daven*. Since he already knew how to study, he decided to travel to Mezritch. Apparently, Rashbatz was referring to this concept in his reply.]

the discourses I heard from the Rebbe, and he also repeated to me the explanatory remarks he himself heard privately."

A complete biography of Rashbatz — describing everything that happened to him during the next half century, 5615-5665 [1855-1905] — would represent a very long chapter in the history of *Chassidus* and chassidim. Such a complete biography is beyond the scope of this periodical, and a short outline will have to suffice. We hope to be able to print — from time to time — supplementary articles with brief stories of his life and reviews of his talks.[22]

In the year 5615 [1855] he went into business as a dealer in *seforim*. This business was very profitable, giving him ample income to cover his household expenses.

During that same year, a son was born to him. When the child was a year old, he became very ill (may All-Merciful G-d preserve us). Rashbatz went to see the Rebbe [the *Tzemach Tzedek*] and give him a *pidyon*. Upon entering, he began to weep, but the Rebbe said to him, "Put your *pidyon* down here."

It was well known that whenever the Rebbe declined to take a *pidyon* from a petitioner's hand, but instructed him instead to put it down on the table, it was not a good omen. All of Rashbatz' begging did him no good, and he had no choice but to lay it on the table. The Rebbe then replied, "it's too late!" Rashbatz returned home in tears, to discover that the child had died.

In the year 5625 [1865] the Rebbe assigned him the task of printing *Torah Or* with the supplementary remarks, and in 5626 he was given *Likkutei Torah* to print. Before he departed, the Rebbe gave him a *pidyon* to take to Mezhibuzh, to the gravesite of the Baal Shem Tov.

---

22. [Unfortunately, publication of *HaTamim* ceased before these supplements could be printed.]

Several wondrous things happened to him during this journey. He related that when he arrived in Mezhibuzh, he somehow became aware that much mercy was needed, and he began to weep from the depths of his heart. He later revealed what the contents of that *pidyon* had been: [the Rebbe petitioned that] G-d would grant him a long and peaceful life, that he would derive spiritual joy from his sons and his family, and that G-d would elevate the fortunes of the Torah and the Jewish religion....

While he was in Zitomir, attending to the printing of *Likkutei Torah*, he learned of the passing of the saintly Rebbe the *Tzemach Tzedek*.[23] He remained there until just before the festival of Shavuos 5626. During the month of Elul, he was traveling near Lubavitch; on the way, he discovered that the holy Rebbe Reb Yehudah Leib was then in Kapust, and so he decided to spend *Shabbos Selichos* with him.[24] He arrived in Lubavitch for Rosh HaShanah of 5627.

In the year 5629 the Rebbe Maharash appointed him a *shadar*, and in that capacity he traveled throughout the counties of Minsk, Vitebsk, Chernigov, and Poltava until the year 5631. [Wherever he went,] he would review chassidic teachings generously.

During the entire year 5631 he remained at home in Lubavitch. At that time he would study *Chassidus* with the [future] holy Rebbe Rashab, twice a week before the morning prayer, from four to six o'clock. On several occasions the Rebbe [Rashab] spoke at length praising the great pleasure he had taken in studying with him, and the many sound interpretations he had given.

---

23. [13 Nissan 5626 (March 29, 1866).]
24. [The Rebbe Maharash had not yet officially succeeded his father as Rebbe in Lubavitch; Reb Yehudah Leib, on the other hand, had already assumed the position of Rebbe in Kapust. Moreover, he had become close to Reb Yehudah Leib upon first arriving in Lubavitch, as described above.]

This study program lasted for three months. However, since the [future] Rebbe also *davened* at great length, and was very diligent in his other studies, [his father] the Rebbe Maharash was afraid that his health would be adversely affected. He therefore instructed him to cease studying with Rashbatz.

After that, Rashbatz resided in Kremenchug, and would come to Lubavitch once a year, or once in two years, to visit his family. In the year 5642 [1882] he came for Rosh HaShanah. On 13 *Tishrei* [September 26, 1882] the Rebbe Maharash passed away, and so Rashbatz remained in Lubavitch until Chanukah. He comforted and consoled the Rebbe's family, for they were all heartbroken and in deep mourning over the great tragedy and disaster that had occurred when the crown of their head (and the jewel of the eye of the entire Jewish people) was taken from them.

In 5644 [1884] he moved to the settlement of Bulhakov along with his family. There, he had twelve students with whom he studied *Gemara* and *Poskim*. On *Shabbos*, he would review chassidic teachings for the local residents.

In 5651 [1891] he moved from Bulhakov to the city of Nicholayev. There too, he studied with the local young men, and some young folk who came there to be with him. [During the week] he taught them *Chassidus* from the printed word, and on *Shabbos* he would review it for them by heart.

In 5653 [1893] the Rebbe [Rashab] requested him to come to Lubavitch and tutor his son.[25] He arrived before Rosh HaShanah of 5654, and remained as his tutor until about 5660 [1900]. Their study was in great depth.

In 5660 he assumed the duties of head *mashpia* of the *Chassidus* curriculum for the class of *bochurim* studying in the

---

25. [The future Rebbe Rayatz.]

Yeshivah Tomchei Temimim in Lubavitch. He retained that position for the rest of his life.

Rashbatz passed away at 11:45 P.M. on *Motzoei Shabbos,* the eve of Sunday, 15 Sivan 5665 [June 18, 1905] and, according to his request, was buried [in Lubavitch] near the burial sites of the Rebbe the *Tzemach Tzedek,* and his son, the Rebbe Maharash (may their souls be bound up in the bond of eternal life).

Reb Chanoch Hendel[1]

By
Reb Schraga Feivish Zalmanov
of Warsaw

Our holy Rebbe[2] told one of the students who was studying diligently in Lubavitch — the "Place of Enlightenment":

> [The *Talmud* says],[3] "Serving [as an apprentice to scholars of] the Torah is greater than studying it." And how does one serve as an apprentice to Torah scholars? By attending *farbrengens* led by elder chassidim such as Reb Chanoch Hendel and others like him.

As is well known, before the holy *Yeshivah Tomchei Temimim* was founded in the year 5657 [1897], the *bochurim* who studied in small groups in Lubavitch were called "the sitters." These were outstanding young men, sons of the chassidic brotherhood of *Anash*. After they acquired a broad knowledge of the revealed Torah — *Gemara-Rashi-Tosafos* and *Poskim* — in their hometowns, they would come to bask in the shadow of our saintly Rebbe, and to hear the words of the Living G-d — the discourses on *Chabad Chassidus* — that issued forth from the Holy of Holies, the mouth of our saintly Rebbe, each week on *Shabbos* eve. Afterwards, they

---

1. From *HaTamim*, Issue No. 1, pp. 79, 80. This short article appeared at the end of the biography of Rashbatz.
2. [Apparently, the Rebbe Rashab.]
3. [*Berachos* 7a.]

would review the discourse until they knew it well and could repeat it by heart, word for word as the Rebbe had delivered it. There were many *bochurim* who knew a hundred or more chassidic discourses by heart. Each thus acquired a broad knowledge of the fundamentals of *Chabad Chassidus*.

In addition, the Rebbe suggested to one of the sitters (when he went in for *yechidus*) that in order to assimilate chassidic qualities and an appreciation of the chassidic way of life in their hearts, they should serve as apprentices to the elder chassidim such as Reb Chanoch Hendel. With this in mind, when the holy *Yeshivah, Tomchei Temimim*, was founded, a course of *farbrengens* with the teachers and *mashpiyim* was established as a regular part of the curriculum.

The chassid Reb Chanoch Hendel[4] was a noble leader among Jews, an elder among those chassidim who chose G-dliness as their heritage, to dwell in G-d's palace in Lubavitch, and to enjoy the aura of the Divine Vision that was the Rebbe. In those days, there were many famous personalities living in Lubavitch, notably the chassid Reb Shmuel Betzalel, known as "Rashbatz," the chassid Reb Abba Czasznyker, and others. Each of them excelled in some aspect of religious practice and personal quality. Rashbatz was renowned for his intellect, Reb Abba for his earnestness, and Reb Chanoch Hendel for his chassidic conduct.

Reb Chanoch Hendel was a chassid — to the very core of his being he was a chassid. His every concern, thought, word, and act were about *Chassidus*, and demonstrated the inner essence of his vitality. His personality was fundamentally very vivacious, and he was therefore able to instill the quality of vitality in all who were close to him. The sages

---

4. Reb Chanoch Hendel arrived in Lubavitch in the year 5603 [1843] or 5605; he passed away there on 9 *Teves* 5660 [December 13, 1899].

said,[5] "Who is a chassid? He who performs *Chassidus*...." In other words, he himself behaves as a chassid, and inspires others to do the same. This was Reb Chanoch Hendel's essential quality.

Each day between *Minchah* and *Maariv*, he would teach *Tanya* to those wonderful young men, the sitters. He did this with an inner essence of vivacity and with fiery fervor, with heartfelt speech that seemed fresh each time one heard it. Anyone who heard these lectures became elevated in stature, and the life-spirit of *Chassidus* entered his inner being. Every story that he employed to illustrate some point in *Tanya* gave new life to the listener. Each time he taught a subject, it was from a fresh perspective.

He would become exceedingly impassioned whenever he told stories about our holy Rebbeim; his face would shine with the radiance of the sun. It was wondrous to behold his attachment to Torah scholars. He especially loved and praised prominent chassidic personages such as the chassid Reb Shmuel Dov of Borisov ["Rashdam"], the chassid Reb Avremke of Zhembin, and the like. He constantly spoke in admiration of their great intellectual abilities, their system of *avodah*, and the open (as well as the secret) miracles they performed. When he described these things, he did so with such remarkable feeling that he transformed the character of all those who listened, and their very beings changed for the better.

Each member of *Anash* was precious to Reb Chanoch Hendel, and he truly loved every one of them with great and eternal love. He rejoiced when they were joyful, and felt personal sorrow at their misfortunes.

---

5. [Introduction to the *Tikkunei Zohar*, p. 1b. The quote is rendered somewhat non-literally here.]

Whenever a member of *Anash* came to see the Rebbe, Reb Chanoch Hendel would go immediately to the home where the guest was staying and greet him personally with a smile, with joy, and in a most cordial manner. Then, with words of surpassing love and adoration, he would show the guest "the way to the Tree of Life."

The first time I had the privilege of witnessing the gracious glory of his splendor was in the year 5655 [1895] between Pesach and Shavuos, when I first arrived in Lubavitch to study. As I recall the occasion, I was studying in the side-room of the Rebbe's *beis hamedrash*, known as the "smaller study hall," studying in depth my lesson in *Gemara-Rashi-Tosafos*. Suddenly, my ears picked up the sound of someone singing a *niggun* so beautifully that it aroused the heart.

Interrupting my studies and turning toward the door of the *beis hamedrash*, I witnessed this marvelous sight: there was a table which stood between the eastern and western walls of the *beis hamedrash*, and at the center of this table sat a man with a most handsome face, wrapped in *tallis* and *tefillin*, and *davening* in a pleasant and melodious voice (with a *niggun* that was well known in Lubavitch). He was reciting the passage *Az Yashir* word by word, his face shining as though he had discovered some priceless treasure. Tears flowed unceasingly from his eyes. This sight reminded me of the statement in the *Zohar*,[6] "Joy is fixed within my heart on one side, and tears on the other side." The whole scene amazed me.

When Reb Chanoch Hendel finished his *davening*, he approached me with a smile and inquired who I was, where I had come from, and what the purpose of my coming to Lubavitch was. I replied that I was related to the local *Rav*,

---

6. [Vol. II, p. 255a.]

and that I had come to study Torah. Upon hearing this reply, he invited me to visit him at his home, and to join his class in *Tanya*.

From then on, he always treated me in his usual friendly fashion and with his great love, showing me the "road that leads to the House of G-d," through which one might adhere to the "Tree of Life," the holy Rebbe. This was his constant habit and the sacred path he followed, bringing souls closer to their Father in Heaven. It is known that the holy Rebbe himself commanded that on Reb Chanoch Hendel's tombstone there should be engraved the words, "He prompted many to turn back from sin;[7] may his merits protect us and all of Israel."

---

7. [Cf. *Malachi* 2:6.]

REB AVRAHAM BER[1]

BY
THE EDITORS OF *HATAMIM*

B.H.

One of the guests who came to Lubavitch for the *bar mitzvah* of the Rebbe [Rayatz] on 12 Tammuz, 5653 [June 26, 1893] was the great chassid, outstanding in both intellectual pursuits and prayer, Reb Avraham Dov Ber, son of Reb Yirmeyah, of Bobroisk. Reb Avraham Dov is remembered with great praise among chassidim. He would speak with hesitance about worldly matters.[2] But when it came to chassidic matters and chassidic stories, he was quite articulate.

He was very tall, and his appearance was imposing. His father, Reb Yirmeyah, was born in Homel; he was a businessman, but also an accomplished scholar. As a young man he had once seen the Alter Rebbe, but his main adherence was to the Mitteler Rebbe and to the *Tzemach Tzedek*. He was also a member of the inner circle of the great Reb Aizik *HaLevi* of Homel.

The chassid Reb Yirmeyah chose the best *melamdim* to educate his son, for he was an apt pupil with outstanding

---

1. From *HaTamim*, Issue No. 2, pp. 120-128; 19 *Kislev* 5696. The editors of *HaTamim* inserted the following introductory remarks at the beginning of the article:
    Some biographical notes concerning [the childhood of] the famous chassid, Reb Avraham Dov Ber of Bobroisk, o.b.m., known as "Reb Ber Yirmeyah's." This essay is based on notes made by one of the students studying in Lubavitch at that time, who heard the whole story from this chassid himself.
2. [An alternative translation: "he stuttered when speaking of worldly matters."]

abilities. The scholars of Homel admitted him to their circle, and when he reached the age of *bar mitzvah*, the *Rav* — Reb Aizik — accepted him as his student. Reb Avraham Dov studied under Reb Aizik for four years, with great diligence. At the age of seventeen, he was brought by his father to the *yeshivah* in Lubavitch for the festival of Shavuos.

[Reb Avraham Ber told of his background]:

My father was quite wealthy; he grew wealthier each year, and he donated large sums to charity. Besides that, my mother went out of her way to cater to visitors and guests in our home. Whenever my father planned a trip to Lubavitch, a lottery was held to determine which of the chassidim would be privileged to accompany my father, at Father's expense.

When I reached the age of six, in the year 5592 [1832], Father took me to Lubavitch for Shavuos, before enrolling me in the *cheder*. Right after Pesach I was told that this year my father would take me to Lubavitch. We began preparing for the trip on Lag BaOmer.

In Homel, a large feast was always held in honor of Lag BaOmer, and Reb Aizik would deliver a chassidic discourse. It was impossible to accommodate all the chassidim and other residents of the town all at once. Therefore, the celebration was spread out over three or four days — sometimes even five or six days.

It was an old custom in Homel to hold a special celebration on the *Shabbos* after Lag BaOmer: This was called "the Joyous *Shabbos*," for the celebration was as joyful as *Shabbos Bereishis*, which follows Simchas Torah. When Lag BaOmer fell on Sunday, the entire week — until after the Joyous *Shabbos* — was celebrated as a festival.

The program for this celebration was as follows: after the *davening*, all the chassidim, the scholars, the affluent businessmen, and the elders would assemble in Reb Aizik's home. There, they discussed what spiritual improvements and what civic improvements were needed in the city, and they drew up a tax assessment to collect money for various purposes. Then they paid a visit to the cemetery, after which they returned to the *beis hamedrash*, where tables had been set up with food for the feast held in honor of the *mitzvah*.

Each day of the festival Reb Aizik would deliver a lecture on *Chassidus*. During that time, the monies were collected for the previously mentioned tax, to support the various projects. Small children were enrolled in the *chadorim* during that season, and the pupils of the intermediate and senior *yeshivos* were examined on their knowledge.

Reb Aizik decreed that when Lag BaOmer fell on Thursday or Friday, the celebration was to continue until after the second *Shabbos*. In 5592, Lag BaOmer fell on Friday of *Parshas Bechukosai*, and so the celebration lasted until after *Shabbos Parshas Bamidbar*. I was thrilled at the time, for I knew that my father was going to enroll me in the *cheder*, and take me to Lubavitch.

I will never forget that pilgrimage — the memory of it remains engraved upon my heart. We departed from Homel in four wagons, each drawn by two horses. There were fifteen passengers in each wagon: some were seated in two rows inside the wagon, some sat along the sides of the wagon, and two sat up above, next to the coachman. Everyone was in an extremely happy mood.

Most of the people traveled on foot; their ecstasy indescribable. They rode in the wagons only for an hour or two at a time to rest their feet. Reb Aizik rode in the lead wagon, along with my father and some other chassidim. I was seated next to my father, just opposite Reb Aizik.

Mother woke me very early Sunday morning, telling me to dress quickly and go to Reb Aizik's house. From there, the holy pilgrimage to Lubavitch would depart. With great joy, my mother packed the new suit she had sewn for me, instructing me to wear it only on *Shabbos*, and when I would be privileged to have an audience with the Rebbe.

We came to the street where Reb Aizik lived — despite the early hour, the street was already buzzing with people hurrying to and fro, as though it were a market day. We arrived at Reb Aizik's home and found the courtyard packed with men, women, and children: some conversing excitedly, some dancing. The four wagons stood ready for the trip.

It was impossible to enter Reb Aizik's home, for it was already filled to capacity, and Mother had no idea where my father was. As we stood there, we learned that Reb Aizik had lectured on *Chassidus* all night, and they had begun the public prayer service at daybreak. The other scholars and wealthy businessmen had just now arrived to escort their *Rav* on his way.

A short while later we heard the sound of music. Suddenly, people began to emerge from the house through the doors and windows. They walked backwards, their faces toward the house and their backs to the courtyard. Everyone in the courtyard began to tremble, and within a few seconds Reb Aizik appeared. He stood there and blessed the assembled crowd, bidding them farewell; then he climbed onto one of the wagons.

Just then, my mother caught sight of my father, as he too climbed onto the wagon after Reb Aizik. She began to shout, "Yirmeyah! Yirmeyah! Here is Avraham Berel. Please take him, please don't forget Avraham Berke," but her voice was lost in the loud confusion. Just as the wagon carrying Reb Aizik and my father began to move, I began to cry, seeing that my father had forgotten about me.

All those in the courtyard raised their voices in song, as they began to follow the wagon. Meanwhile, Mother noticed Reb Yisrael Aharon the *melamed* among the crowd, and she informed him that father had left me behind, and had not heard her when she called him. Reb Yisrael Aharon lifted me in his arms and, forcing his way through the multitude, he carried me to the wagon where my father sat.

The wagon proceeded very slowly, as the host of people accompanying us increased. At each intersection, hundreds more joined us. Before our escort from Homel had a chance to turn back and return home, a party from the town of Belitza appeared. They had come to welcome our procession, which would be passing through their city. In Belitza, Reb Aizik descended along with father and the other travelers. However, I was afraid that my father would forget me once again, and so I remained in the wagon to await their return.

Our journey from Homel to Lubavitch lasted five days, from Sunday to Thursday of *Parshas Naso*. We passed through many cities and towns, villages and rural settlements. Wherever we went, there was rejoicing and celebration. On the way, we were joined by other wagons headed for Lubavitch from Bobroisk, Szczedryn, Smilian, Toltchin, Minsk, Borisov, Zhlobin, Shklov, Rogatchov, and many other places. Many foot travelers also joined the procession. We were scheduled to arrive in Dubravna Wednesday at *Minchah* time.

Our last stop before that was to be in Zaliszkina, fifteen or sixteen miles from Dubravna, where the wealthy chassid Reb Eli Moshe lived. When we arrived in Zaliszkina, we found many — at least twenty or thirty — wagons, with hundreds of people resting on the grass in the open field across from the courtyard of Reb Eli Moshe.

Tens of groups of people were scattered all over the place: some engaged in conversation, some sleeping, some eating and drinking, some reviewing a chassidic discourse, some dancing. I held tightly to Father's coat, so that he would not forget me.

The wealthy chassid Reb Eli Moshe, his sons, sons-in-law, wife, daughters, daughters-in-law, grandsons, granddaughters, brothers, sisters, and all their kin, had their hands full as they labored to serve the assembled chassidim who were on their way to Lubavitch. They provided food and drink for everyone, free of charge.

The chassid Reb Eli Moshe used to say, "Ninety-nine percent of all that Heaven bestowed upon me because of the Rebbe's blessings, belongs to the chassidim; only one percent belongs to me. So, friends, eat and drink! It is the Rebbe's blessing that you are eating, and I give it to you in token of our great friendship. Eat, drink, and be merry! Be strong chassidim, with the energy to serve G-d through Torah and *mitzvos* and the *avodah* of the heart."

In Zaliszkina, we met the two famous chassidim, the *tzaddik* Reb Hillel of Paritch and the chassid Reb Betzalel of Ozaritz. Their great joy at meeting Reb Aizik is indescribable. The three of them ate lunch together in Reb Eli Moshe's home. When we left Zaliszkina, forty additional wagons joined us, along with many companies of foot travelers. Most of them carried knapsacks on their shoulders and walking sticks in their hands. Some of them had good voices, and sang as they walked. Those riding in the wagons joined the chorus with great joy.

Our journey proceeded among the tall trees of a vast forest. The sound of music could be heard in the distance, as each stanza of the song echoed through the forest. The effect was as if a choir of singers was positioned at the edge of the forest, repeating whatever we sang. Finally, I spied sunlight in the distance, indicating that the forest was ending. Inside the forest, the daylight was obscured by the thick branches, as though it were twilight.

A few moments later we emerged from the dense trees into a broad open field. Before us stood a huge mountain, upon which the sun shone brightly. All of us who were riding in the wagon — except Reb Aizik, the elderly *tzaddik* Reb Yechiel ben Reb Meir "the tearful one," and the *gaon* Reb Zalman Dov "the milkman" — got off the wagon to walk until we reached the mountain top. From the mountain's peak we could see the gardens and homes of the city of Dubravna, still more than two miles away.

As we went down the mountain, we saw a large crowd of people standing along both sides of the road. We soon learned that the chassidim of Dubravna — led by the famous chassid Reb Nechemiah — had come out to greet the guests who were on their way to Lubavitch.

After we reached the Dubravner Chassidim assembled at the bottom of the hill, Reb Aizik descended from the wagon and went to meet the *tzaddik* Reb Nechemiah. My father accompanied him, after appointing the wagon driver Reb Avraham Meir to keep an eye on me, and ordering me to obey his instructions to the letter.

I was exhausted from the trip, and soon fell fast asleep; thus, I knew nothing of our arrival in Dubravna. When I finally awoke, Reb Avraham Meir was already finishing his breakfast. He informed me that we would be resuming our journey within an hour or two, and would arrive at nightfall.

On Thursday toward evening, we finally arrived in Lubavitch.

On Friday afternoon, about an hour before sunset, the large *shul* was already packed wall-to-wall with people. On the platform in the center stood the Rebbe's sons and a few other dignitaries and elder chassidim, including Reb Aizik. Suddenly the word spread: "The Rebbe is coming!" Instantly there was silence, all eyes focussed on the place where the Rebbe would enter.

I was standing on top of one of the stoves, holding Reb Avraham Meir's hand. In a moment, I saw a man dressed in white silk, with a fur hat on his head, proceeding toward the platform. He sat in the chair prepared for him, and began to speak in a powerful voice: "And G-d spoke to Moshe: Count the numbers of the sons of Gershon too...."[3] (This is the second discourse on that verse which was later printed in *Likkutei Torah*).[4]

I remember well how I went in to the Rebbe with my father for *yechidus* on that occasion. Father had to wait in the outer room for many hours, until it was his turn to enter. Meanwhile, I sat on a widow ledge. When the time appointed for our audience arrived, my father asked the people standing near me to hand me over to him. I was passed hand-to-hand over the heads of the assembled chassidim.

Father entered the Rebbe's inner chamber, and I followed him, holding tightly to the corner of his coat. The room in which the Rebbe sat was quite large, the walls lined with cabinets full of *seforim*. The Rebbe sat behind a large table, upon which lay a few *seforim*, several boxes filled with coins, and two lit candles.

---

3. [*Bamidbar* 4:21-22.]
4. [Pp. 46-49.]

As Father entered the chamber, the Rebbe was studying a *sefer* which lay open before him. But when we approached the place where the Rebbe sat, he raised his eyes from the *sefer* and gazed into father's face, and into mine. Father's entire body began to quake, and I also became flustered and began to weep silently

The Rebbe stretched out his holy hand to take the *pidyon* from my father, as father stood in his place, paralyzed with fear and at a loss for what to do next. He remained standing in silence, his head bowed, his eyes running rivers of tears which fell to the floor. At first he managed sufficient self control to keep from being heard, but within a few moments he broke into loud weeping, his voice wailing up and down the scale. When I saw Father crying like that, my heart went to pieces and I too began to cry in earnest as I looked into the Rebbe's holy face.

The Rebbe read the *pidyon* that father had handed him, and studied it for some time. As he read it, he looked up into father's face, and into mine, from time to time. Then he began speaking to Father. As soon as the Rebbe began speaking, Father ceased his weeping. He moved his lips silently, repeating every word the Rebbe spoke, but making no sound. The Rebbe continued speaking to Father for a long time; then Father asked him several questions, which the Rebbe answered.

When the Rebbe finished speaking, Father said, "Here is my son," as he pointed to me and moved me closer to the Rebbe. "I am about to enroll him in the *cheder*, and I beg the Rebbe to bless him."

The Rebbe studied me for a moment, then he closed his holy eyes. After a few moments he opened them again, looked directly at me, and said, "Study diligently, and do not waste any time. May G-d (blessed be He), help you to become a scholar and a chassid."

"*Amen!*" Father and I both exclaimed.

As soon as we emerged from the Rebbe's holy presence we went to the small *minyan* room. Father lifted me onto his shoulders and began to dance with the chassidim who were already rejoicing in song and dance. This was the usual custom in those days: whenever someone had the privilege of *yechidus* with the Rebbe, he would break into a dance upon leaving the holy chamber.

Father continued dancing for a very long time, until his clothes became soaked with perspiration, as wet as if they had just been removed from the laundry tub. Afterwards, he sat down on one of the benches in a corner of the *shul*, to rest a bit. "I must rest for a while," he said, "but soon we will go the home where our *Rav* is staying."

I perceived that Father was in a joyful mood — though completely exhausted, he continued clapping his hands and stomping his foot to the rhythm of the dance. From time to time he would snap his fingers, or whistle a piercing, high-pitched note that refreshed the spirits of those who were weary from dancing, giving them renewed energy to dance even faster.

I was always fond of joyous occasions in general, and dancing in particular. My earliest memories are of chassidic dances. That was at the time I first began to crawl; I could only do so on all fours, but could not yet stand up. Whenever someone held me in a standing position, or placed me in my infant's walker, I would cavort about in imitation of the dances I observed in my father's home. As soon as I began to walk and talk, my first words were to shout that I wished to join the chassidim in their dancing.

One of Mother's favorite activities was entertaining guests, especially when a chassidic *farbrengen* was involved. The chassidim who were Father's close friends came to our home frequently for study and conversation. Afterwards they would begin a dance. I always joined in, while holding on to the corner of the jacket of one of the dancers.

Among those who took part in the *farbrengens* and dances there were two young men — the youngest in the whole group — who were very lively individuals. They were talented singers, and their voices could be heard above everyone else's. They were also swift dancers, and whenever they broke into a dance they would lift me onto their shoulders. Sometimes Anshel Gitte's would carry me, and sometimes Shlomo Peshe's would carry me; either way, I thought I was the luckiest fellow in the world.

I used to refer to our *farbrengens* as "Little Simchas Torahs." When I was three years old, I began to attend the kindergarten class of Reb Elimelech the children's teacher. There, I would play with the other children in my class, and we heard stories from the *Chumash*, Prophets, and *Aggadah*. I would say to my friends, "Yesterday (or the day before) we had a Little Simchas Torah at our house."

All of my little friends (sometimes even the older children, who were already reading Hebrew from the *Siddur* or *Chumash*) envied me. I was exceedingly proud, for I was the only one in my class who frequently had an opportunity to attend a Little Simchas Torah. What's more, to ride on the shoulders of those jolly young fellows — Anshel Gitte's and Shlomo Peshe's — while they danced their wonderful dances, was a privilege enjoyed by no other child but me.

I loved to taunt my classmates about this, especially little Schneur Zalman Dov, the son of the chassid Reb Aryeh. He in turn, would taunt me, for I was only named after my maternal grandfather, who had died quite young, while [Schneur Zalman Dov] was named after both the Alter Rebbe and the Mitteler Rebbe. But whenever he gave me his verbal abuse, I reminded him that I could get a ride on the shoulders of Reb Anshel and Reb Shlomo while they danced.

I once asked my mother why it was that the chassidim — who spent so many hours conversing and *farbrenging* — were always so joyful, dancing and prancing about. She replied that they — the chassidim — had been sitting and studying; they rejoiced with the Torah knowledge they had thus acquired, which constituted a "Rejoicing of the Torah." It was after this that I began to refer to these events as "Little Simchas Torahs."

Being accustomed to Little Simchas Torahs, I was not surprised by the vigorous dancing of the chassidim in the little shul. But why did they make it a point to dance specifically after they emerged from the Rebbe's holy presence? Furthermore, why was such an audience in the Rebbe's private chamber called *yechidus*? For example, one might ask another, "Were you in *yechidus* yet?" To this, the reply might be, "I am just about to go in to *yechidus*," or "Thank G-d, I have just been in *yechidus*." One might also hear remarks such as "so-and-so went for *yechidus*," and "so-and-so is waiting for *yechidus*."

My mind became totally preoccupied with these two questions: a) why is entering the Rebbe's private chamber called *yechidus*? b) why do chassidim begin dancing when they emerge from the Rebbe's chamber? This preoccupation gave me no rest, and when I noticed that my father was in such a good mood, I asked him my two questions.

Father asked me: "Do you know about the *Mishkan* that Moshe built in the wilderness according to G-d's command? Do you know about the special chamber that was there, in which the Holy Ark with the Tablets stood? Do you know that once a year, on Yom Kippur, Aharon the *Kohen Gadol* would enter that chamber to light the incense and to pray for all of Israel?"

Being eager to show off my erudition to my father, I quickly recited everything I knew about the Temple that King Shlomo built, about the Most Holy Chamber with the Ark and the Tablets, the sacrificial service performed by the *Kohen Gadol* on Yom Kippur, and especially his entry into this innermost chamber. When the *Kohen Gadol* pronounced G-d's holy Name, all the people in the Temple courtyard would kneel and bow, touching their faces to the ground.

As I spoke, I proudly demonstrated to Father how they bowed and fell on their faces. For the past two years I had been in *shul* on Yom Kippur afternoon, and when everyone in *shul* had knelt and bowed, I had copied the grownups. Upon rising from my bowing, I had run to tell Mother about it; she then gave me a slice of white bread without butter, explaining that it was a holy fast day.

"Who entered the Most Holy Chamber together with the *Kohen Gadol* on Yom Kippur?" asked Father?

"Only the *Kohen Gadol* — no one else!" I replied.

"And what did the *Kohen Gadol* do after he completed the sacrificial service of the holy fast day of Yom Kippur?"

"Our teacher, Reb Elimelech, told us that the *Kohen Gadol* was very wealthy, for he wore golden garments, made from his own personal gold. When he completed the service in the *Beis HaMikdash*, he would go home accompanied by all the Jews, with song and melody. When they arrived at his home, there were tables laden with all sorts of food and drink. Everyone joined in the most joyful celebration, for their sins were forgiven."

"And now," asked Father, "do we have a *Beis HaMikdash* and a Most Holy Chamber?"

"No," I replied with a sigh, "Now we have neither a *Beis HaMikdash* nor a Most Holy Chamber."

I looked up at my father, waiting to hear what he would say next about all of this. But before I could regain my voice, a new group of people entered the *shul* singing, and another dance broke out. When father realized that most of the men in this group were our townspeople from Homel, he suddenly sprang up from his bench with outspread hands and jumping feet, and joined their dancing.

I was startled by this, and didn't know what to do. My first impulse was to follow my father, but I was afraid I might be trampled under their feet. I retreated, and climbed up to stand on one of the benches. I noticed the wagon driver Reb Avraham Meir among the dancers, but when I called his name he didn't answer.

I stood on the bench and watched, as father danced in the middle of the circle. All around him were several of the Homeler Chassidim, among them Reb Avraham Meir the wagon driver and Reb Shlomo Peshe's. Each one danced with closed eyes, his right arm on his neighbor's shoulder, his left arm waving to the beat of the sacred melody issuing from his mouth. An indescribable aura of holiness surrounded the dancers' faces. The love and brotherhood, the bliss and the ecstasy, are unimaginable. Each one held his neighbor tightly, in friendship and harmony. I nearly burst apart with desire to join the dance.

Reb Avraham Meir passed me by a second time, and then a third. Each time, I called to him, but he didn't respond. But suddenly, someone seized me from behind. I felt myself flying through the air, and there I was riding on the shoulders of one of the dancers. Bending my head forward, I discovered that Reb Shlomo Peshe's was carrying me on his shoulders. My rapture knew no bounds!

In a thunderous voice, the chassid Reb Zalman Yaakov Esther-Disha's (a leading citizen of Homel, he was the *gabbai* of the *shul* and was intimately involved in all affairs of the community and its institutions) suddenly cried out, "Here ends the first *hakkafah*! Now it's time to *daven Minchah*."[5] Within seconds of this announcement the dancing ceased, and everyone got ready for *Minchah*.

Father's words about the *Beis HaMikdash*, the Most Holy Chamber, the Ark, and especially his last question, "And now, do we have a *Beis HaMikdash* and a Most Holy Chamber?" had left me somewhat sad and dejected. In my mind, a new question began to take shape: why was everyone so joyful, if the *Beis HaMikdash* remains destroyed and goats[6] cavort in the place where the Most Holy Chamber once stood?

The men in the *shul* began *davening Minchah* in melodious tones, each one showing off his vocal talents; they *davened* loudly, in the Simchas Torah style. Meanwhile, my thoughts were busy with my new question — why are they so happy while the *Beis HaMikdash* remains destroyed? At the same time, I recalled all the stories [about the destruction of the *Beis HaMikdash*] our teacher Reb Elimelech had told us on the previous *Tishah BeAv*. I therefore decided to ask Father to explain it all to me after he finished *Minchah*.

When the *davening* ended, Reb Zalman Yaakov Esther-Disha's announced that liquor and cake were being served. I then turned to Father and said, "You asked me whether we still have a *Beis HaMikdash* and a Most Holy Chamber. Well,

---

5. [These rituals imitate those customary in the *shul* on Simchas Torah during *Hakkafos*.]
6. [Another translation: "demons." Cf. *Yeshayahu* 13:21.]

nowadays we have neither, so why is everyone dancing so joyfully? After all, the *Beis HaMikdash* is destroyed, and goats caper in the Most Holy Chamber!"

When Father heard this question he replied, "You are right, my son, you are very right. The *Beis HaMikdash* that stood in the Holy City of Jerusalem (may it be speedily rebuilt) is now destroyed. When the Jews do *teshuvah*, then the Holy One (blessed be He), will send us *Mashiach*, our righteous redeemer, who will gather us from the four corners of the earth and take us — together with our houses and our furniture — to the Land of Israel, where he will rebuild Jerusalem and the *Beis HaMikdash*. Until that time, we have neither the *Beis HaMikdash* nor the Most Holy Chamber. In the meanwhile, Lubavitch is our Jerusalem, the *shul* where the Rebbe *davens* is our *Beis Mikdash*, and the room where the Rebbe sits is our Most Holy Chamber. The Rebbe himself is our Holy Ark containing the Tablets of G-d's Holy Torah."

Father's solemn facial expression as he spoke these words made an awesome impression on me. Then, the realization struck me: Father and I had just been inside the Most Holy Chamber, and we now found ourselves in the *Beis HaMikdash*. What an wondrous idea! Very awesome indeed!

As these thoughts about the *Beis HaMikdash* and the Most Holy Chamber went through my mind, I heard Father speaking to me again. "Are you aware, my son, that after Moshe deposited the Ark and the Tablets in the Most Holy Chamber, he was able to hear G-d's voice speaking to him from between the *Ceruvim* on top of the Ark?"

"Yes," I replied, "I heard Mother reading about this to my aunt."

"The words that the Rebbe speaks to each chassid entering his chamber for *yechidus*, are the word of G-d," father continued. "Just as the *Kohen Gadol* used to enter the Most Holy Chamber all alone, so too, whoever enters the Rebbe's room (which is now our Most Holy Chamber) does so all alone. That's why the audience is called *yechidus*.[7] And just as the *Kohen Gadol* and all of Israel rejoiced when he emerged from the Most Holy Chamber, so too, we chassidim all rejoice and celebrate the great kindness that G-d has shown us by giving us the privilege of entering our Most Holy Chamber and receiving our Rebbe's holy blessing. Remember well the words of the blessing the Rebbe gave you," Father cautioned me. "G-d willing, when we get home, you can tell Mother all the details."

Before I could reassure my father that I remembered the Rebbe's blessing, and was able to repeat it word-for-word, Reb Zalman Yaakov Esther-Disha's approached us. He made Father go to the table and partake of the liquor and cake. He gave me a sweet biscuit with some jam on it; I recited the blessing of *Mezonos* out loud, upon which my father and the others who were near enough to hear my blessing answered "*Amen.*"

Reb Abba David the *Chazan* and Reb Baruch Shimon the Bookbinder congratulated father for having the good sense to bring me to Lubavitch. "You were very wise to bring your Avraham Berel to Lubavitch," said Reb Abba David. "These days, it's necessary to train the children in *Chassidus* from early childhood."

"If you ask me," remarked Reb Baruch Shimon, "It was his wife's clever idea, not his own. She is a truly wise woman, a real chassidic woman, who is always entertaining guests."

"I too, entered the Most Holy Chamber, along with my father, and the Rebbe blessed me," I related, as I looked at

---

7. [*Yechidus* means "private" in Hebrew.]

Father to see whether I was permitted to tell them the words of the blessing I had received from the Rebbe. But Father was busy in conversation with the men on the opposite side of the table.

Just then, Reb Shlomo Peshe's came running in drenched with perspiration, and announced that all the chassidim who had come from Homel had already been in *yechidus* (thank G-d). They were now *davening Minchah*, and would arrive here very soon.

"For bringing such good news, you deserve a glass of liquor and some cake," Reb Zalman Yaakov Esther-Disha's said to Reb Shlomo Peshe's, "Here it is, so take it, say the blessing, then say *LeChayim!*"

Reb Shlomo Peshe's recited *Mezonos* over the cake, and *Shehakol* over the liquor; then he blessed the whole assembly with *LeChayim*, his face all golden and radiant. After he drank, he began to clap his hands, sing, and dance while standing in his place.

He turned to his audience and asked in bewilderment, "Have you been sitting motionlessly like this the whole time, eating and drinking but not dancing? I am well aware of what a big chassid Reb Zalman Yaakov Esther-Disha's is. Our *Rav* says of him that he has a great deal of common sense, but his frigid disposition and his strict etiquette are intolerable. If you follow his example, you will all wind up like white geese — fattened geese that waddle about with great dignity and crow in orderly unison.

"Brothers, we get enough of his manners and etiquette at home in Homel. Here in Lubavitch, our Holy Jerusalem, we are liberated from the yoke of the authorities on etiquette, who look to the *misnagdim* for guidance, and pay attention to what direction the wind blows, worrying about what people will say."

"Just look at that!" exclaimed Reb Abba David the *Chazan*. "Now he too has become one of the speakers. When we were still young, we never dared to open our mouths and speak at a chassidic gathering, let alone voice our opinions out loud. Believe me, Shlomo, it takes real impertinence."

"Times have changed!" said Reb Gershon Leib the Scribe. "In our days we behaved very differently. Young folk knew their place, and their only duty was to listen and pay attention when elder chassidim spoke among themselves."

Turning to Reb Meir Yechiel the Fisherman, Reb Gershon Leib continued, "Do you remember the first time we went to the Alter Rebbe in Liozna?"

These two — Reb Gershon Leib the Scribe and Reb Meir Yechiel the Fisherman — were older chassidim, in their seventies or more. Reb Gershon Leib had already retired from writing Torah scrolls, *tefillin*, and *mezuzos*, and Reb Meir Yechiel had retired from fishing, but they retained the names of their former occupations. They now had ample income from their real estate holdings, and they played a leading role in all charitable affairs (according to their means). They held great prestige among all factions of the community, for they spent the entire day and most of the night in *shul*, studying Torah and *davening*.

By nature, Reb Gershon Leib was the silent type. He used to say that his occupation was a holy one, and his work had to be done with the proper intent and the proper frame of mind, and required much patience. Thus, over the years, the virtue of patience had become his second nature, and he had become accustomed to thinking rather than speaking.

When Reb Gershon Leib began to speak, there was complete silence, and everyone present lent an ear to hear what he had to say. Reb Gershon Leib's story is very long, but all the chassidim of Homel knew it by heart. Quite frequently, when there was a *farbrengen* Reb Gershon Leib would retell his beloved story (or at least part of it).

It would take me too long to give all the details of what I wrote down about this trip to Lubavitch. But when I arrived home I told my mother everything that had happened to us, and everything that I saw during our journey and in Lubavitch. I also repeated the Rebbe's blessing. I became extremely diligent in my studies after returning from Lubavitch. My *melamed* was quite satisfied with me, and delighted in teaching me. For my second semester, Father transferred me to the second grade *melamed*.

During the next four years, the Rebbe's instructions, "Study diligently and do not waste any time" resounded in my ears, along with his blessing, "May G-d (blessed be He), help you to become a scholar and a chassid."

Father and Mother took great pleasure in my diligent study and my G-d-fearing behavior. By the age of ten I had already acquired a great deal of *Talmudic* knowledge, and father again took me with him to visit Lubavitch.

Then too, I accompanied him in to the Rebbe for *yechidus*. After he finished speaking to Father, the Rebbe gazed intently into my face, and then said to Father, "I can see in his face that the has studied diligently."

He turned to me and inquired about what I had studied. I replied that I had studied the tractates *Beitzah*, *Bava Kamma*, and *Bava Metzia*, and I was now up to the second *Mishneh* of the Chapter entitled *Makom Shenahagu* ["In the place where it is customary"] in the tractate *Pesachim*. In *Tanach* I had studied *Chumash* with the commentary of *Rashi*, and the Early Prophets.

The Rebbe meditated for a while and said, "What you have studied until now is good. For the future, finish the tractate *Pesachim*, and then study *Bava Basra* and *Nedorim*; *Shulchan Aruch Orach Chayim*; the weekly portion of *Chumash* with the commentaries of *Rashi*, *Or HaChayim*, and *Panim Yafos*; *Tehillim* with *Rashi's* commentary, and then the Later Prophets. May G-d help you to dedicate yourself to diligent Torah study and fear of Heaven, and may you be a scholar, a chassid, and a G-d-fearing person."

During the next three years, from the age of ten until my *bar mitzvah*, I completed the tractates of *Pesachim*, *Bava Basra*, and *Nedorim*, as well as reviewing *Bava Kamma* and *Bava Metzia*. I knew these tractates, along with the commentaries of *Tosafos*, thoroughly.

When Father took me to Lubavitch for my *bar mitzvah*, I had the privilege of receiving a blessing from the Rebbe, while he placed his holy hands upon my head. Unfortunately, I was unable to hear the words of the blessing.

When I returned from Lubavitch, Reb Aizik admitted me as a student at the third table of the *yeshivah*. A year later he promoted me to the second table, and a year after that to the first table. At the age of seventeen I was accepted as a student in the second class of the Rebbe's *yeshivah* in Lubavitch. This class was taught by the holy Rebbe Reb Yisrael Noach,[8] and we were examined by the holy Reb Levi Yitzchak,[9] the Rebbe's son-in-law.

---

8. [A son of the Rebbe the *Tzemach Tzedek*; he later served as Rebbe in Niezhin.]
9. [He was married to Rebbetzin Devorah Leah, daughter of the *Tzemach Tzedek*.]

Reb "Y.M."[1]

COMPILED BY THE EDITORS OF *HATAMIM*,
FROM THE PREVIOUS REBBE'S DIARY

Petersburg, Tuesday 11 *Shvat*, 5672 [January 30, 1912];
Hotel Estari, Room no. 527; 11:30 A.M.

I have just now arrived on the Paris-Petersburg express. This train travels along the French and Italian coasts, along the following route: Paris, Marseilles, Nice, Monte Carlo, Menton, Ventimiglia, Genoa, Frankfürt, Berlin, Königsberg, Kovna, Petersburg. I spent about two hours in town, and informed all my associates that I had arrived. However, I am exhausted from the trip, and I also desire to record what occurred during my travels. Therefore, I told my associates that we would not meet until nine o'clock this evening.

---

1. From *HaTamim*, Issue No. 3, pp. 88-93; 2 & 13 *Nissan* 5696, and continued in *HaTamim*, Issue No. 4, pp. 80-85; 12-13 *Tammuz* 5696. The editors of *HaTamim* inserted the following introductory remarks at the beginning of this article:

    In this issue, instead of our usual feature — biographies of famous chassidic personalities — we present a fascinating narrative of a descendant of a great and famous line of chassidim. For various reasons, he strayed from the path of observant Judaism for several years (may we be spared such a fate), having been swept along with the tide of secular life. Thanks to a certain event ordained by Divine Providence, he was reunited with his origins and became an observant Jew, faithful to G-d and His Torah.

    Several versions of this story have been disseminated among chassidim, and factual errors have crept into it. Therefore, we thought it advisable to petition the Rebbe [Rayatz], *Shlita* to provide us with notes from his personal diary that refer to this incident. The Rebbe consented to our request, and we herewith present excerpts of these notes, rearranged in chronological order.

I traveled by express train in a private compartment. In fact, all the compartments on this train were for single occupants. The train left Paris on *Motzoei Shabbos Parshas Bo*, the eve of Sunday 9 Shvat, at 11:30 P.M. Upon entering my assigned compartment, no. 3, I discovered that it was furnished with a table and chair in addition to the bed, and a wash-room that was shared with the adjoining compartment. There was also a bright lamp, which led me to believe that I would be able to do some writing. But when the train started to move, I found that its speed made it impossible to write more than a few sketchy notes, and even this entailed some difficulty.

We arrived in Marseilles Sunday, 9 Shvat, at daybreak. The train stopped there for ten minutes, and then resumed its journey. The porter informed me that we would make stops of fifteen minutes each at the stations in Monte Carlo, Ventimiglia, and Bordegheri, while the stops in Nice and Menton would each last half an hour. While the train traveled along the coast, it would do so at a slower pace, so the travelers could enjoy the natural splendor of the scenic view.

My saintly father the Rebbe, and my mother the Rebbetzin, were in Menton at that time; therefore, I looked forward to our arrival in Menton with special anticipation. When I had left Paris for Menton on Monday, the third of this month (as mentioned previously in this diary) it had been agreed that Father would come to the station to receive a report of my activities in Paris, and to give me instructions for my forthcoming communal endeavors in Petersburg and Moscow.

At nine-thirty the train arrived at the Menton station. Before the train came to a full stop, I already saw my father sitting in a chair in the station lobby, for the large windows afforded a wide view of the tracks. As soon as the train stopped moving, I hurried into the large station lobby.

As we met, Father's face beamed with his usual soft and gracious smile that uplifts and inspires the heart. We exchanged greetings for a short while, and then I reported everything I had done in Paris. I began with a description of my visit to [...], and ended with the final meeting that had taken place *Motzoei Shabbos* at seven o'clock in my hotel room number 223, "Hotel Garre du Nord," and the decisions we had arrived at.

Father was pleased with the results of my trip, and presented me with a schedule for further communal work. He approved my agenda, which entailed remaining in Petersburg for no more than a day and a half. During this time there was to be a meeting with [...] and I was to visit [...]. On Thursday morning I would be in Moscow, and that evening I would return home to Lubavitch by way of Smolensk and Krasnoye. On Tuesday 3 Shvat I was to attend the convention in Kiev, on Monday and Tuesday (1 and 2 Adar) I was to participate in the convention in Petersburg, and on 7 or 8 Adar I would return to Menton with a detailed report.

The porter approached and informed me that the train was scheduled to depart in a few minutes and I should return to my place. Father gave me his blessings for a successful journey, and I hurried back to the train while he remained in the station lobby. He went over to an open window, and when the train began to move he spread out his hands in a gesture of blessing, as the *Kohanim* do. Fifteen minutes later we were in the Ventimiglia station at the Italian border, and from there our journey continued.

The trip along the seacoast was very beautiful; [indeed] the wonderful feelings evoked by this glorious scenery really deserve to be recorded in full. Unfortunately, time does not permit this, and I will only describe my impressions of a chance meeting with a chassid of the M. family who — for various reasons — had experienced a progressive spiritual descent (may we be spared such a fate). But Divine Providence arranged things so that he would not remain lost, and could rehabilitate himself.

The M. family as a whole was descended from a distinguished Jewish lineage — especially the chassidic branch of the family. The patriarch of the clan, named Reb Shlomo, had been born in the city of S., the descendant of an important family. G-d had blessed him with sons and daughters, and with a large business in the diamond and jewelry trade. His chief income came from the large cities of Petersburg and Moscow, and he frequently traveled to Paris, Antwerp, and Amsterdam to purchase his diamonds and jewels.

Reb Shlomo was a fervent chassid, and as a young man he had visited the Mitteler Rebbe, who had given him a threefold blessing: for many sons and daughters, great wealth, and long life. His son, the chassid Reb M. M., once told me a long story explaining why his father, the chassid Reb Shlomo, had been found worthy of receiving this threefold blessing. It is recorded in my diary of the year 5661.

Reb Shlomo engaged chassidic *melamdim* to educate his sons. Whenever he traveled to my great-grandfather, the *Tzemach Tzedek,* he would take his sons along with him. When they were of marriageable age, he arranged matches with wealthy chassidic families of his own kind, and he took his sons into his business as partners, for the business was constantly expanding.

In time, his sons and sons-in-law also became heads of large families, with many sons and daughters of their own, and they founded their own companies in the diamond and jewelry business. This wealthy chassid Reb Shlomo lived a very long life, and his descendants were prominent both in chassidic circles and in the diamond and jewelry trade.

At six o'clock, I entered the dining car to drink a cup of tea while reading several urgent letters given to me by my father in Menton. At one of the tables sat an elderly Jew eating his dinner, which included [unkosher] meat and wine. As soon as I entered the car, the man put on his hat and approached me, extending his hand in greeting of *Shalom Aleichem!* "Are you the son of the Rebbe Maharash, or perhaps his grandson?" he inquired.

My first impulse was not to answer him, for I was quite upset with this person who ate unkosher food. But since his facial expression was very gracious, I quickly changed my mind. "Yes," I replied, "I am the grandson of the Rebbe Maharash of Lubavitch."

Upon hearing my reply, his face grew red and his eyes filled with tears. Without another word he returned to his table, summoned the waiter, paid his bill, and departed without finishing his meal.

At eleven o'clock that evening, the train arrived at the station in Frankfürt am Main, where it stopped for some time. I got off the train for a breath of fresh air, and I noticed that this person had done likewise, and was now walking toward me. He approached and said that he would like to tell me an interesting story. He was quickly overcome with emotion, and tears flowed from his eyes, rendering him unable to speak. Meanwhile, the time arrived for the train to depart. I entered my car, and he entered his.

Early the next morning we arrived in Berlin. When I got off the train for some air, the man approached me again and wished me "Good morning," complaining that he had been unable to sleep a wink all night.

When the train left Berlin, I stood up to *daven*; there had been no opportunity to do so earlier, as it was still before daybreak. Before I finished my prayers the porter entered my compartment and informed me that one of the passengers wished to come in and visit me. I instructed him to apologize for the delay, and to inform the man that he would be able to enter in half an hour.

At the appointed time the person entered and apologized for disturbing me. "I am so overcome with emotion that I am unable to speak," he said. He began weeping loudly, which made a great impression on me. The man appeared to be over fifty years old, and was dressed in elegant fashion. His beard was shaven, and his moustache was curled in an ornate style. Suddenly, without a word, he covered his face with his hands and broke into bitter tears.

I was confused by this scene, not knowing whether to attempt to comfort him or to let him be. As I was watching him, his whole body shuddered; I thought that perhaps he had gone mad, or that some other misfortune had occurred to him. Unable to bear it any longer, I began to comfort him. Within a few moments he began to speak in a trembling voice, "Do me a spiritual favor — please lend me your *tefillin*."

I could scarcely believe my ears: what he was requesting was the favor of lending him my *tefillin!* Before I could question him further, he exclaimed, "*Ach, mein G-t!* I have no idea how many years it's been since I last put on *tefillin*," and he wept unceasingly.

I opened my suitcase, took out my *Rashi tefillin*, and gave them to him, saying that he could *daven* in my compartment. I left the compartment, allowing him to pour out his heart before G-d undisturbed. He continued *davening* for quite a long time. When he finished, I entered the compartment and he returned the *tefillin* to me with profuse thanks, asking to borrow my *Siddur*. I assumed that he wished to say some *Tehillim*, and to use the *Siddur* when he *davened Minchah*.

He then returned to his own car, without telling me who he was. It was evident that the man had undergone some inner turnover, but I still had no idea who this person was or what had happened to him.

At three o'clock in the afternoon, the porter came to me again, relating that the same passenger who had visited me that morning now wished to see me again. I gave my consent, and he entered my compartment. His face was white, and had a very sad expression. In a weak voice, as though he were ill, he began to speak.

Mr. Y. M.'s story:

My name is Mr. Y.M., and I am the son Reb Leib M., who was born in the city of S., and was one of your grandfather's chassidim. During my childhood and adolescence, I studied in *cheder*, and was taught by the finest *melamdim*, who were chassidim and men of good deeds. The chassidim would assemble in my father's home on every chassidic festive occasion, and I was, of course, one of the first to attend.

Eventually, however, my father moved from S. to Petersburg. It is true that even there his lifestyle was based on the principles of Torah and *Chassidus*, and even there chassidim regularly gathered in his home. However, I was influenced by the children of our various neighbors, and began to follow in their ways.

One day toward the end of summer, while we were living at our vacation home in a suburb of Petersburg, Father told me that when he traveled to Lubavitch for the coming Rosh HaShanah, he planned to take me with him. I was then about fifteen years old, and I had already sampled the lifestyle of the neighboring youths, who accepted no restrictions to indulging their appetites. Obviously, I had no relish for Father's plans to take me to Lubavitch.

When the time came, my father set off for Lubavitch along with two other chassidim, taking me along too. About ten other people, members of the well-known chassidic A., A., and T. families, joined our party. Five or six others, whose expenses were paid by the wealthy K. Brothers, also traveled to Lubavitch.

Seeing the face of your grandfather the Rebbe made an indescribable impression on me. When I entered his chamber together with my father for *yechidus*, he gave me an explicit blessing for success in everything I did. But he cautioned me to remember that I was a Jew, for the company I was presently keeping was quite hazardous.

The impressions of my trip to Lubavitch affected me for a long time after our return to Petersburg, and stopped me from associating with the sons of our gentile neighbors. To their great surprise, I even refrained from joining their festivities and games during their holiday season, which I had done in previous years. This situation continued until the next summer, when we again moved to our vacation home.

When we were in our summer home, I was already a high school student, and little-by-little I began to associate with my young contemporaries. Some of them were scholarly and possessed refined qualities, while others sought a life of pleasure. But all of them influenced me to estrange myself from the lifestyle followed in our home.

On one occasion I came home late, and failed to *daven Minchah* and *Maariv*. Another time, being in a hurry to join my friends in swimming, I skipped *Shacharis*. On a third occasion, I ate with them. Thus, over the summer months, I abandoned the religious way of life to which I had been accustomed in my father's home.

When we returned to the city from our country home, Father began to prepare for his annual Rosh HaShanah trip to Lubavitch, but I remained at home. I remember it as if it were today: when I went to *shul* during Rosh HaShanah and Yom Kippur, the whole scene seemed foreign to me.

During the gentile holiday season, I spent all my time with my non-Jewish friends, rarely coming home. Once, when I did come home, it was to see my mother and ask her to give me a few hundred rubles. Twice, I visited my father's office to ask his cashier for some money that I needed.

When the holiday season ended and I returned home, Father admonished me and said that he was ready to give me as much money as I needed. But he demanded that I sever all my ties with my young friends, the delinquent schoolboys. I replied that I was already grown up, and would live as I myself chose, for my parents had no right to interfere with my private life.

To demonstrate my independence, I left my parents' home, and found myself an apartment of my own. Thus, the next six years passed. I finished high school, got married, and led the totally secular life I had chosen for myself, almost completely forgetting my former lifestyle in my father's home.

At that time, a society was founded, called the "Young Progressives." The goal of this society was to champion the cause of the oppressed and the downtrodden, to look into their well-being, and to afford them moral and material support. A major part of the society's efforts was devoted to the economic situation of our fellow Jews.

One day, in December 1881, I met an acquaintance who told me that the Lubavitcher Rebbe was visiting Petersburg, and had gone to see several high government officials with whom he had discussed the economic situation of the Jewish people.

Being a member of the Young Progressives (as I have mentioned), I was curious to find out what your grandfather had accomplished in the community's behalf. For this purpose, I went to Hotel Serapinsky in Zablakonsky Street, where your grandfather was staying.

When I arrived at the hotel, I met numerous chassidim whom I had not seen for many years — since leaving my father's house. They were overjoyed at seeing me; for the first time, I became aware of the warm love chassidim have for their brethren, even for those who have gone astray.

I then remembered the uproar that had ensued in Father's home during the first few days after I moved out and went to live in my own apartment in Pushkinsky Street with a few of my young friends. Before my eyes I saw once again — as though it were happening at that very moment — two of my father's friends, who had visited me and entreated me to return to my father's home. I had been overcome by their display of love and affection toward Father and me, as they had wept passionate tears in sympathy with father's distress.

I had no doubt that over the years they had spoken of me from time to time, and had inquired about my lifestyle. I am certain that knowing my lifestyle caused them inner pain. Nevertheless, when they met me at the entrance to the hotel, they greeted me with open arms and warm regards, as if I was one of their number.

The chassidim possess a unique quality: love for their fellows, without regard to rank or standing. It makes no difference to them whether one is poor or rich, elderly or young. This quality places them on the highest ethical level.

More than once, we nonobservant young folk spoke among ourselves about this quality of love for one's fellow, and how we ought to take an example from the chassidim in this regard.

This meeting in Hotel Serapinsky affected me greatly, and left me with a warm feeling that words cannot describe. As I stood there daydreaming about the old days, I was startled by the sudden sound of voices crying, *Baruch A-donai hamvorach leolam vaed*.[2]

At first I had no idea what this was, but I quickly realized that they had begun to *daven Maariv*. Your grandfather the Rebbe emerged from his room and recited the last *Kaddish* following *Aleinu*, because that day happened to be the *yahrtzeit* of the Alter Rebbe, author of the *Tanya*.

It took three days for me to calm the emotions aroused within me by that meeting with my old acquaintances from the days of my youth. I was even more overcome by the *Kaddish* I heard your grandfather recite, for it reminded me of the time I had spent in Lubavitch.

On January 4, we members of the Young Progressives discovered that the Minister of Internal Affairs had hinted to the governors of Kiev, Czernigov, and other territories, that they were to instigate pogroms against the Jews. We knew that your grandfather had come to Petersburg on communal business. The main focus of his trip was the pogroms that had begun in the southern regions, and the wave of anti-Semitism that was then sweeping the country.

We were also aware of his great influence in government circles, and that he had explicitly and forcefully demanded that the Jewish citizens of the country be defended. We

---

2. ["Blessed be the L-rd, Who is blessed for ever and ever," the opening response of the *Maariv* prayer, recited by the congregation in response to the *chazan*; p 106 in the *Siddur*.]

therefore decided to send several of our members to share our information with your grandfather.

However, we also knew that your grandfather was reserved, and that he was not fond of (to put it more accurately, he despised) the secular youth. Therefore, it was quite likely that he would refuse to listen to us, or he would require us to reveal the sources of our information and to present him with convincing proofs of it. Since I was a leading member of the Party, and the head of the Jewish Affairs Division, I was selected to visit your grandfather accompanied by one other member, and to reveal to him what we knew.

When we arrived at Hotel Serapinsky we could think of no excuse for requesting an audience with your grandfather — we couldn't reveal the purpose of our visit in advance, and we were sure that we would not be admitted without stating our purpose. However, we learned that it was your grandfather's habit to take a walk at nine thirty every morning. Therefore, we decided to wait for him in the hallway; when he passed by, we would hand him a note stating that we had an important matter to discuss with him, and wished to make an appointment.

The next morning we arrived at the hotel at nine o'clock as we had decided. To our disappointment, we discovered that he would not be taking his walk that day, for two high officials of the Ministry of Internal Affairs had an appointment to see him at eleven. We were glad to learn of this meeting, for your grandfather could make good use of our information when he spoke with them. But we still had no plan for obtaining an audience.

As we stood there bewildered, the door suddenly opened and your grandfather emerged, accompanied by the wealthy chassid N. H. They began to pace back and forth along the hotel corridor, while my colleagues and I remained in the far corner. A few moments later your grandfather happened to raise his eyes, and he noticed me. Though he had not seen me for eight years (and I don't have to tell you that my appearance had changed considerably during that time), he immediately recognized me. He inquired about my welfare, and asked whether I still remembered the chassidic discourse I had heard in Lubavitch.

I was so surprised, that I became flustered and was unable to utter a word. Seeing my confusion, my companion said, "We have an urgent matter to discuss with you, Rebbe." Your grandfather returned to his room, and ordered the wealthy chassid N. H. to invite us to enter.

I will never forget the penetrating gaze that your grandfather fixed upon us; such a glance leaves an everlasting impression. From that morning on, my companion and I became your grandfather's aides in his endeavors to quell the anti-Semitic sentiments that were then spreading among the government officials and ministers.

There is much that I could tell of your grandfather's activities during the month he spent in Petersburg; through his great influence, he succeeded in suppressing several evil decrees against the Jews.

One day, while I was visiting your grandfather, he suddenly turned to me and asked, "How long has it been since you stopped putting on *tefillin*? Don't try to deny it! I don't need anyone to inform me about it. I can tell you everything you've ever done, and exactly when and where you did it."

As I sat there in amazement trying to think of some reply, he began to recite to me, incident by incident, everything that had happened to me, and the steps by which I had gradually abandoned the Jewish religion. I was struck dumb, my head began spinning, my heart palpitated, and rivers of tears ran from my eyes.

For the next several days, I was too ashamed to appear before your grandfather, but eventually I received a note from the wealthy chassid N. H., informing me that your grandfather had asked about me several times. I then went to visit him, and he assigned me several tasks of public service to perform.

The previous conversation with your grandfather had such an effect upon me that the following morning I obtained a pair of *tefillin* (I had left my own *tefillin* in my father's house when I moved out). Keeping it a secret from my family, I began to put on *tefillin* and *daven*, and I avoided eating anything but bread and tea.

During the first week I offered various excuses, saying that I was sick and unable to eat. But eventually I was forced to reveal to my wife that I had resolved not to eat unkosher meat anymore. With great difficulty I managed to stick to a kosher diet, and to adopt a few other features of the Jewish way of life.

Your grandfather left Petersburg and returned home to Lubavitch. After that I began to live a more religious life, but I didn't visit my father, nor was he aware of the changes in my lifestyle. In the middle of April I moved to our summer home in the Petersburg suburbs together with my wife and my oldest son.

A few days later my father came to visit me; this visit astounded me, for I had no idea why he had come. To my great surprise, Father handed me a letter written to him by your grandfather. The letter contained an invitation to the wedding of one of his sons; in the margins, he had included a note of greeting to me, indicating that I too was invited to the wedding. "Did you have to trouble yourself personally?"

I asked Father. "You could have had it delivered by one of your office workers."

"When the holy Rebbe writes a letter to someone, we chassidim do not entrust it to workers; such a mission must be carried out promptly and precisely," Father replied. "I have no idea why — or in reward for what good deeds — you have been privileged to receive greetings from the holy Rebbe, and an invitation to join his joyous celebration. But since the Rebbe did in fact write to you, who will dare to question the king? I received the letter today, and I immediately set out to fulfill my mission. Having done so, I now bid you goodbye!" he concluded, as he prepared to return home.

It took a great deal of effort for my wife and me to convince him to remain for a few hours, so that we could have a cup of tea and take a walk in the woods together. Father told me about the forthcoming wedding of the Rebbe's son, and I in turn filled him in on the highlights of my conversations with your grandfather when I had seen him during his visit to Petersburg the previous winter. I described the zealous and unyielding manner in which he had dared to address high government officials, while expressly demanding justice and fairness in no uncertain terms.

We had been in conversation for three hours when we suddenly heard someone calling, *Shalom Aleichem!* and saw the chassid Z. R. walking toward us. He greeted Father very warmly, and also greeted me with a big smile. He then recited the blessing of *Shehechiyanu*. Father and I looked at him in surprise, for we could not guess why the chassid Z. R. had recited the blessing.

"Why are you looking at me like that?" asked Z. R. "In the Alter Rebbe's *Seder Birchos HaNehenin*, it clearly says that whenever something causes a person some special joy, he must recite *Shehechiyanu*, mentioning G-d's Name and Majesty. Now, when I saw you, my dear Leible, strolling lovingly with your son Y. — and having heard from Avraham the butcher that for the past half year he purchases his meat from him exclusively — I was overjoyed at seeing him, and so I said the blessing *Shehechiyanu*."

The three of us continued walking silently for a short while, until Z. R. broke the silence saying that many of the chassidim were planning to travel to Lubavitch for the wedding celebration. Finally, we returned to my home, where my wife had prepared supper. Father wanted to return to the city, but the chassid Z. R. begged him to eat something with us. He too joined us for supper; we ate with much enjoyment, and from then on, peace was restored between my father and myself.

On June 20, your grandfather arrived in Petersburg and remained there for two weeks. He worked diligently and accomplished much for the public benefit. On August 6 the central committee of the Young Progressives met to discuss the poor economic status of the Jews in the southern towns. It was decided that a special emissary should be sent to your grandfather to inform him of the present situation and to request his aid; this mission was assigned to me.

I arrived in Lubavitch early in the morning of August 8. Knowing that your grandfather was in the habit of rising very early, I immediately went to the Rebbe's courtyard and handed the *gabbai* a note addressed to him. Within half an hour I was summoned to the Rebbe's chamber. I gave him a full report, and he questioned me closely about every minute detail.

After about two hours he interrupted the meeting, saying that because of his poor health he had to take a ride in the country twice a day: at nine thirty in the morning, and at six thirty in the evening. Therefore, he was forced to interrupt our meeting, but we would meet again before eleven o'clock.

When I emerged from your grandfather's room, I caught sight of his coach, to which two grand horses were harnessed. On the driver's platform sat the coachman dressed in his uniform, with a red sash at his waist and a feathered cap on his head, like the coachmen of the nobility.

At ten thirty I reappeared at the Rebbe's court, but he had not yet returned from his ride. I went to the *beis hamedrash* to wait for him, and hundreds of eyes gazed at me while my ears caught fragments of conversation concerning me. People were making all sorts of guesses about the purpose of my visit, but no one was bold enough to approach and speak to me, other that a few who wished me *Shalom Aleichem!*

Meanwhile, the door opened and a newcomer entered the *beis hamedrash*. Everyone present immediately became very excited, and all hurried over to the guest with exclamations of *Shalom Aleichem!* while many of them exchanged kisses with him. An atmosphere of friendship and love prevailed.

I was very intrigued by the expressions of love and joy on everyone's face at seeing this man, and so I turned to one of the men and inquired who he was. I was informed that he was none other than the *shadar*, Reb Gershon Dov. "Don't you recognize the *shadar* Reb Gershon Dov?" he asked innocently.

I must confess that at the time I had no idea what *shadar* meant, and I was about to inquire, when the *gabbai* Reb Leivik approached. I remembered Reb Leivik well from my first visit to Lubavitch with my father, but he apparently didn't recognize me. "The Rebbe has sent for you," he said, and with undisguised annoyance he added, "There are about five hundred guests waiting for audiences, including some who have been here since before *Shabbos*. Therefore, kindly do not take up too much of the Rebbe's time."

Your grandfather's face appeared pale as he greeted me. "I have just come from the *Ohel*," he said. "My father — the holy Rebbe the *Tzemach Tzedek* — says that the situation is not so severe, but that we must nevertheless do something."[3]

He spent over an hour with me, outlining a program of communal work for me to carry out, with whom I was to meet, and what I was to discuss with each. He requested that I take brief notes; when he saw that I was writing in Russian, he said, "That's not such a good idea! Nowadays, young folk need to be more careful, for there are many eyes following every step they take."

When he finished speaking, he wrote two letters in Russian: one addressed to Professor B., and the other to Lord Z. He asked me to check the grammar so that the recipients would not misunderstand the contents, and then he gave me the letters.

He was silent for a few moments, after which he turned to me and said, "When Moshe went up on High to receive the second set of Tablets, the Holy One said to him[4] '*Engrave for yourself* ....' *Rashi* interprets it to mean that 'The residue will belong to you.'[5] As you know, the residue left over from cutting precious stones in also quite precious, and one can become very wealthy from it. By this means, the Holy One taught us a lesson in life: if a person is occupied with doing good deeds, he must be rewarded for it. Now you are occupied with public service, and you too deserve a reward."

---

3. [This took place sixteen years after the *Tzemach Tzedek* had passed away!]
4. [*Shmos* 34:1.]
5. [A play on words: the Hebrew words for "engrave" and "residue" have a common root פסל.]

He then began to explain to me what this means in spiritual terms. "When I said to you that I had just come from the *Ohel*, and that my father says that the situation is not so severe, I noticed that you laughed to yourself. Now this was not because you don't believe in spiritual matters; it is because you are so immersed in the material world that you have lost all awareness of spiritual matters."

Your grandfather continued speaking to me for a long time, and he told me many stories. In conclusion, he said, "bear in mind always that reward exceeds punishment. Concerning Yishmael — who was an uncivilized person — the *Midrash Rabbah*[6] (quoted by *Rashi* on *Chumash*[7]) says, 'If you throw a branch into the air, it will return to its place of origin.' How much more so must this be said about a chassid who is a descendant of chassidim! He must surely return to his origins.

"How long can a person stray! Fifty, or perhaps fifty-five years. Hot blood and lust also have a limit. Remember who you are, and don't forget from where you have grown. May G-d watch over you and grant you good fortune. Tell your father that I wish to see him soon."

When I left his presence, there remained an hour and a half until the train to Vitebsk and Petersburg was to depart from Rudnia Station. In the meantime, I would have to travel by coach from Lubavitch to Rudnia Station. I arrived at Rudnia Station ten minutes early, my limbs aching from the ride in the coach.[8]

The ticket agent refused to sell me a ticket for the full trip to Petersburg. He claimed that there was not enough time

---

6. [*Bereishis Rabbah* 53:15.]
7. [*Bereishis* 21:21.]
8. [Rudnia is the location of the closest train station to Lubavitch, and the road between Lubavitch and Rudnia was unpaved and very rough. It has not improved very much to this day.]

for him to calculate the mileage from there to Petersburg and the proper fare for it, and to write the ticket. He was not accustomed to figuring such large sums, and would sell me a ticket only as far as Vitebsk. No doubt the ticket agent in Vitebsk was used to calculating larger sums, and would sell me a ticket all the way to Petersburg.

"From here in Rudnia," said the agent, "No one travels as far a Petersburg except the Lubavitcher Rebbe. And in such cases, they notify me several days in advance, and I prepare the ticket. When he arrives, I merely fill in the date, and stamp it."

When I arrived in Denenburg, I got off the train and entered the station house to get a cup of tea. There, I discovered that the police were inspecting travelers' papers, and even searching the baggage and the pockets of some of them. Stacks of papers lay piled on a table, and several officers sat there reading through them.

I remembered your grandfather's words about taking necessary precautions, and I began to think of ways to avoid the inspection — or at least to find an inconspicuous corner where I could tear up your grandfather's two letters, and my notes on the communal activities he had assigned to me. But a moment later I made up my mind that I would behave like a veteran chassid; I remained confidant that they would certainly not search me. I summoned the waiter and asked him to bring me a glass of cognac to put in my tea.

There remained two hours until the train departed for Petersburg. During that whole time they continued searching the belongings and the papers of the travelers, including those who were seated at the tables. The only ones they skipped were several high officials who were in uniform. Although the policemen passed to and fro before me innumerable times, they never approached me. I was convinced that this must be a miracle.

When I took my seat in the train, I found out that several people had been arrested; some had been sent to the Denenburg prison, while others had merely been detained pending further investigation. No one knew the reason for all this, and I did not discover it until I arrived in Petersburg, where my friends were already worried that I too had been arrested.

At a secret meeting, I reported to my colleagues all that your grandfather had suggested, and his agenda for improving the economic situation of our fellow Jews. When I told them about the two letters, and all that had transpired in Denenburg, they were quite amazed.

The day after my arrival, I visited Father and told him (in total secrecy, of course) that I had visited your grandfather. I did not tell him what had been said to me about my personal affairs, but I told him that the Rebbe wished to see him as soon as possible. "Two weeks still remain until Rosh HaShanah," said Father. "I had planned to travel to Lubavitch on Sunday of *Selichos*, but I will now make the trip a few days earlier, and arrive in Lubavitch before *Shabbos Selichos*."

The two letters to Prof. B. and to Lord Z. opened the doors of high government officials for me. Within three weeks we had completed all our work with total and unexpected success. Everything worked out exactly as your grandfather had predicted.

When I saw my father after Rosh HaShanah, he informed me that he had traveled to Lubavitch right after *Shabbos*, but the Rebbe had been sick when he arrived. He had spoken with him briefly several times, but his illness grew worse from day to day. Father planned to return the day after Yom Kippur to visit him again.

The painful news about your grandfather's passing reached Petersburg on Tuesday, September 4,[9] at noon, and it caused quite a storm among all segments of Jewry. Even the *misnagdim* and the nonobservant Jews bemoaned the loss of this great man. We members of the Young Progressives held a meeting where we too lamented the passing of the great prince of the Jews.

I remained under the impact of your grandfather's spiritual influence for another year. The central committee of the Progressive Party was disbanded, and a Revolutionary Party was founded in its place. I was not as heavily involved in this party as I had been in the Progressive Party. But my sentiments lay with them, and I made financial contributions according to my means, and lent a minimal amount of personal assistance. Little by little I once again abandoned the religious way of life, until I was completely assimilated and behaved exactly like a gentile.

December 27 is my birthday; I always celebrate the day together with my friends and acquaintances, and I host a grand party in one of the fancy restaurants in Petersburg. But during the past five years — since my wife passed away — my circle of friends, and my wealth, have grown. I therefore decided to begin holding these parties in one of the resort places abroad, and to invite all my friends to travel together and have a good time.

This year I decided to travel to Monte Carlo, then to Nice for a few days, and then to Paris. My friends agreed, and we

---

9. [In the year 1882. This is apparently a printer's error; the correct date should be September 14 in the Old Style Calendar then used in Russia, which corresponds to September 26 in the New Style calendar. This date corresponded to 13 Tishrei 5643, the date of the Rebbe Maharash's passing.]

visited these places. Afterwards my friends returned home, and I remained in Paris for a few days.

The night before last, I left Paris on this train to return home to Petersburg. Yesterday, as I sat in the dining car, I raised my eyes and saw your face; I was immediately reminded of the face of your grandfather, just as he appeared when I last saw him. I recalled his words, "If you throw a branch into the air, it will return to its place of origin."

This very year, I have reached the age of fifty-five. All evening and all night your grandfather's words echoed in my ears: "For how long can a person stray! Fifty, or perhaps fifty-five years. Hot blood and lust also have a limit. Remember who you are, and don't forget from where you have grown." I was unable to sleep a wink. Today I have fasted — not a morsel of food entered my mouth. I regret the lifestyle I have led until today.

[The Previous Rebbe's diary continues]:

He began weeping profusely, and it was with great difficulty that I managed to pacify him. Since he had been fasting, and the time for *Maariv* had already arrived, I urged him to go and get something to eat. But he refused, and instead continued his story.

Y. M.'s story took three hours (with a few short recesses) to tell. Before we parted, he said, "No doubt you will be willing to lend me your *tefillin* tomorrow too. When I arrive home, I will get myself a pair of *tefillin* that very same day, and I will change my ways. I will become a faithful Jew and do as your grandfather commanded me. I will remember that I am a Jew, and will be mindful of my origins."

As he spoke these words, I observed that he was overcome with emotion. We parted in great friendship, and his story continued to affect me for a long time afterward. For almost thirty years, from 5642 to 5672 [1882-1912], the G-dly fire of my holy grandfather's words had remained hidden and concealed within the man's heart, while he wallowed in the filth of pleasure and lust. But finally, the One Who causes all things to happen, caused events to evolve in this way. By means of a certain event, the G-dly fire of the words of *tzaddikim* who live forever caused the spark to burst into a burning flame, inspiring him to return to G-d with his whole heart.

How wondrous are the ways of Divine Providence! The Holy One, blessed be He, ordains a chain of events to support those who have fallen, and to lend a helping hand to those who have rebelled, by showing them the path they should follow.

It is written,[10] "The L-rd is good and righteous, therefore He guides the wicked on the proper way." Commenting on the verse, the *Midrash* relates:[11] "Why is He good? Because He is righteous. And why is He righteous? because He is good."

How numerous are Your kind acts, O L-rd! Yesterday, he fed upon a cauldron of unkosher meat and reveled with bottles of idolatrous wine. But today he is fasting, and has returned unto G-d. As he torments his body, he prays that from now on he will change the course of his life and live as a faithful Jew.

Petersburg, Wednesday, 12 Shvat, 5672 [January 31, 1912]

At five o'clock, Mr. Y.M. called me. I was not in my room at the time. He left a message that I return his call. I called him twice, but he was not at home.

---

10. [*Tehillim* 25:8.]
11. [*Midrash Tehillim* on the above verse.]

Moscow, Thursday 13 Shvat 5672 [February 1, 1912]:

At about eleven o'clock I arrived here at Hotel Bolshoi Sibirsky, room 74. Yesterday at nine thirty in the evening I telephoned Mr. Y.M.

He was thrilled that I had complied with his request that I call him, and informed me that yesterday he acquired *tefillin* and a *tallis* as well as a *Siddur, Chumash,* and *Tehillim,* and that he was carrying out his plans for his new lifestyle. He wished to continue the conversation, but I informed him that I had to travel to Moscow on the train leaving at eleven at night, and I still had much work to do before that.

Kissingen (Germany), Tuesday 23 Menachem Av 5672 [August 6, 1912]:

Today I met Mr. Y.M. for the first time since we parted six months ago in Petersburg. We greeted each other with much joy, and made an appointment to meet again either this evening or tomorrow morning.

Kissingen, Thursday 25 Menachem Av 5672 [August 8, 1912]:

Wednesday at one o'clock the Stolliner Rebbe *Shlita* visited me, and at four o'clock I visited the Alexander Rebbe *Shlita*. Therefore, I was unable to meet with Mr. Y.M. until today. I completed my therapeutic routines early today, and from two o'clock in the afternoon until eight in the evening we strolled together, while I listened with interest to what he told me.

The essence of his story is that when he returned to Petersburg he was unable to endure the company of his friends, and he therefore decided to travel to Menton for a few days. He spent the festival of Pesach in Frankfürt am

Main, and then returned to his home in Petersburg for a month. His friends noticed that some inner turnabout had taken place within him.

Later, he had moved to his summer home, and then had come here to Kissingen, arriving two weeks ago. From here he planned to return home, and to spend the month of Tishrei either in Frankfürt am Main or in Amsterdam.

Moscow, Thursday 14 Teves 5675 [December 31, 1914]:

Today, while walking along Nicholski Street, I met Mr. Y.M. He was very happy to see me, and I, in turn, was pleased to see him. He told me all about himself: His business affairs were prospering, and he was planning to move to some other country. He had not yet decided which country, but it would be a place where he would be able to lead a religious life without hindrance.

Rostov on Don, Tuesday 22 Tammuz 5678 [July 2, 1918]

Today, Mr. Z. Z. told me that he has just come from Petersburg, where the manager of Bank Sibirsky had informed him that Mr. Y.M. has settled in Amsterdam. He also managed to transfer all his wealth: cash, negotiable securities, and holdings in gold and jewels.

Berlin, Wednesday 6 Kislev 5688 [November 30, 1927]:

Today, as I sat in the hotel lobby with my son-in-law Rashag, a bearded gentleman approached me and greeted me with great joy. He was surprised that I failed to recognize him, but when I looked at him carefully I still had no idea who he was.

"Don't you remember when we traveled together from Paris to Petersburg?" he asked. In that instant, the entire scene replayed itself before my eyes.

"The only excuse I can offer is the same excuse Yosef's brothers had for not recognizing him,"[12] I replied.

"Yes," he said, "but besides my beard, all other aspects of my life are also in keeping with what the *tzaddik* your grandfather demanded of me." He told me all that had happened to him, and how he had settled in Amsterdam where he now led a fully religious life without hindrance.

New York, Wednesday 17 MarCheshvan 5690 [November 20, 1929]:

Today I was visited by Mr. C. K. of Amsterdam. During our conversation he informed me that several of our acquaintances from Petersburg have settled there, and he spoke very highly of Mr. Y.M. He described his charitable acts and his financial support of Torah scholars.

Y.M. now leads a life of wealth and serenity on a large estate which he purchased there. He also founded a synagogue, where several *minyonim daven* daily. He himself attends the prayer services every morning, and often comes for *Minchah* and *Maariv,* and to hear the Torah lessons studied between *Minchah* and *Maariv* and following *Maariv*.

Warsaw, Thursday 17 *Teves* 5694 [January 4, 1934]:

Today I was informed by Mr. M.M. that Mr. Y.M. of Amsterdam has become ill. He comes to *shul* only on *Shabbos*, but his home is still open for Torah scholars to visit. "I would never have believed that Y.M. could change so radically," said M.M. "I remember that in our home we were reluctant even to speak his name because of his wicked

---

12. [When his brother's had last seen him, Yosef was seventeen years old and had no beard. Twenty-two years elapsed before they saw him again. He then had a beard, and therefore they were unable to recognize him (*Bava Metzia* 39b, quoted by *Rashi, Bereishis* 42:8).]

ways. But now, one might even confer the title *tzaddik* upon him."

Marienbad, Thursday 7 *Elul* 5695 [September 5, 1935]:

Today I was informed that during the past month of Sivan Mr. Y.M. passed away, following a lengthy illness. May his soul be bound up in the bond of eternal life.

Rashdam[1]

**COMPILED BY THE EDITORS OF *HATAMIM*
FROM THE PREVIOUS REBBE'S DIARY AND LETTERS**

The chassid Reb Shmuel Dov Ber of Borisov was well known among *Chabad* Chassidim, both for his outstanding comprehension of *Chassidus* and his lofty *avodah*. I myself saw him when I was a young lad of seven, and I remember well his features, his appearance, his gestures, and his voice. My saintly father [the Rebbe Rashab] referred to Reb Shmuel Ber as "HaRashdam" (an acronym for "HaChassid Reb Shmuel Dov Ber MiBorisov").

He was tall and thin, with a large head and wide forehead. His face radiated nobility of character; he had large, black eyes that expressed wisdom and strength. He possessed a low-pitched voice, and when he spoke, he would enunciate his words in an unusually pleasing manner. By the time I knew him, he had already grown old, and his hair and beard were white.

As I have mentioned, I first saw him when I was seven years old, during the summer of 5647 [1887] in Lubavitch. My father and I returned from our journey to Yalta, in the Crimea, on *Rosh Chodesh Sivan* 5647 [May 3, 1887], and on our return we found Rashdam in Lubavitch.

In the house of my father the Rebbe, there were two rooms whose windows opened to the garden behind the house; one was my room, and the second was a guest room used by Rashdam whenever he visited Lubavitch.

---

1. From *HaTamim*, Issue No. 5, pp. 99-103; 19 Kislev 5697.

I saw how much honor my saintly father gave to the guest who was living with us in the room next to mine, and I was impressed by his stately appearance. I had already become familiar with numerous honored chassidim whom I had met in Kharkov, while we stopped over there on our way home from Yalta. Therefore, I was bold enough to request our honored guest to tell me some chassidic stories.[2]

Rashdam remained in Lubavitch for seven weeks, during which time I heard many stories from him. I remember most of them to this day. He left for Vitebsk on the day after the fast of the seventeenth of Tammuz;[3] my saintly father traveled with him, and I accompanied them as far as the train station in Rudnia. From there, I returned to Lubavitch in the company of the butler, Mordechai Zilberbord.

The day of their departure remains engraved in my mind because of a certain incident that occurred. When I entered his room on the seventeenth of Tammuz to hear some stories from him, he admonished me for not fasting that day; none of my excuses did me any good. The very next day he left Lubavitch. I never saw him again, but father spoke to me often about Rashdam, praising him greatly each time.

As a child, I was always fond of listening to stories (as are all children). Being an only child, I had been brought up lacking nothing. Nevertheless, I was never mischievous, and at the age of three I already obeyed all instructions to the letter. There were two reasons why I had developed an uncommonly strong love of hearing stories.

[The first reason came as a result of the following incident]: One *Shabbos* night, when Mother was away from

---

2. [To improve the flow of the text, the next few paragraphs were rearranged from their original order.]
3. [A communal fast day, commemorating the fall of the city of Jerusalem to the Romans.]

home in Vitebsk, I entered Father's room and sat down on one of the chairs. I gazed into my saintly father's holy face as he sat at his desk. Several *seforim* lay open in front of him, and his face beamed as he studied them. This sight aroused my jealousy, and I approached the bookcase, took out a few *seforim*, and began to leaf through the pages. But I had no satisfaction from this activity, and I closed the *seforim*, emitting a deep sigh.

I don't remember the exact date, but I believe it was early in the evening of a winter *Shabbos*. My saintly father closed his *seforim* and instructed me to get dressed. He too put on his winter *Shabbos* cloak, lifted me in his arms, and carried me to the home of my grandmother, the saintly Rebbetzin Rivkah. Father exchanged a few words with her, but I was unable to understand what he said. Then, he turned to me saying, "Stay here with Grandmother, and listen to the stories she tells you. Sit quietly, and listen to everything she says. Remember, you've been warned!" He then turned and departed.

My saintly grandmother was then in the middle of reading a large volume, the *Tz'enah UR'enah,* and she read to me the following wonderful story:

> Once upon a time, there lived a man named Terach, who made idols of stone, which he sold to people who would bow down to them. This man had a young son named Avram, who was a wise lad. The son broke all the idols with an iron axe, and then placed the axe into the hand of the largest idol of all. When Terach returned home, he was shocked to find all the idols destroyed. Upon investigation, he discovered that no one had been at home except his son Avram. Turning to Avram, he inquired what had happened.

"A certain woman came here," answered Avram, "bringing a loaf of bread, some meat, and fish, as an offering to the idols. Being very hungry, the idols attacked one another, until the largest idol overpowered them all."

Terach realized that his son Avram was responsible for the damage, and he referred the matter to the court. Since the child was still very young, he was imprisoned until he grew up. Avram remained in prison for ten years, and even there he admonished the idol worshipers for bowing to idols of wood and stone. He told them that there is only one G-d, Who is the King over the whole world and everything in it.

In the land of Kasdim, Abram's birthplace, there was a very large furnace. During the ten years of Abram's imprisonment, this great furnace was continuously stoked, day and night; then they threw Avram into it. But Avram, who believed in the One G-d Who created heaven and earth, strolled about inside the furnace among the flames, as though he were walking among fruit trees in a delightful orchard.

The story spread very quickly: the young Avram — the one who had smashed his father's idols and had been imprisoned for ten years — had been thrown into the fiery furnace, but had remained alive and was walking around inside the furnace. Men, women, and children came by the thousands to see this marvelous sight. This Avram was the very first Jew in the world.

This story captured my heart, and from then on I would come every week after *Shabbos* candle-lighting to visit my grandmother the Rebbetzin. She would always read from her large text, and tell me wonderful stories.

[The second reason why I was so uncommonly fond of hearing stories was]: My first *melamed* was Reb Yekusiel the kindergarten teacher, who was a descendant of famous chassidim. He made it a rule that each day before dismissing the class, he would gather all the pupils and tell them a story about the Baal Shem Tov or his disciples, repeating each story several times. The stories told by my grandmother Rebbetzin Rivkah and my teacher Reb Yekusiel instilled in me a great desire to hear stories.

Rashdam used to say that it was thanks to the chassid Reb Mordechai Horodoker[4] that he too became a chassid.[5] At the age of thirteen, he was brought to Minsk to study. Being a child with great aptitude, he was admitted to the senior *yeshivah* and he was assigned "days,"[6] to eat with families of Torah scholars. He studied in the Minsker *Yeshivah* for four years, and before he returned home (a small village near Borisov), his parents instructed him to stop over in Czasznyk and spend several weeks there visiting his maternal uncle.

When he arrived in Czasznyk, he discovered a large group of young men studying *Chassidus* with great diligence. This amazed him, for though he was already seventeen years old, and a descendant of chassidim, he knew nothing of the teachings of *Chassidus*.

Sunday, 12 Sivan 5659 [May 21, 1899], my saintly father the Rebbe repeated to me the first lesson in conduct that the

---

4. [One of the most honored chassidim of the Mitteler Rebbe.]
5. [See the Prologue and Appendix C of the text *"The Making of Chassidim,"* Sichos In English, Brooklyn, 1996 where these stories are related at length.]
6. [It was the custom to assign *yeshivah bochurim* to local families who would host them for meals; usually, a different family was assigned for each day of the week. This custom is known in Yiddish as *essen teg* ("eating days").]

chassid Rashdam of Borisov had heard from his chassidic mentor, Reb Mordechai Horodoker, the *mashpia* of Czasznyk; it was a lesson that had been taught by the [Mitteler] Rebbe.

"The [Mitteler] Rebbe once said: 'What is forbidden, is forbidden. What is permitted, is not necessary.'[7] We young folk lived with this lesson three or four years," Reb Mordechai continued, "until this ideal had permeated every aspect of our lives. Only then did we go to the Rebbe for *yechidus*."

Here I transcribe — from my diary — a story told by the chassid Reb Meir Mordechai Czernin, that he heard from Rashdam himself.

"When I arrived in Czasznyk," Reb Shmuel Dov related, "I discovered a large group of young men, as well as some elderly men, studying *Chassidus* with understanding and diligence. After I had come to the large *beis hamedrash* a few times, to study *Gemara* in the Minsker style, some people approached me to discuss what I was studying. In those days my haughtiness was still quite evident whenever I discussed Torah studies, and I was eager to demonstrate my prowess with *pilpulim*.

"But the young folk soon made me sweat! They called me appropriate names, and within a week's time they stripped off the gross hide that I had grown in the Minsker *Yeshivah*. Some young men began to befriend me and to study *Chassidus* with me. A new world opened up for me and I began laboring with my greatest abilities; every word was precious to me. Eventually I was admitted to the circle of Reb Mordechai *Mashpia*."

---

7. [I.e., even things not actually forbidden by the Torah should be avoided, unless they are absolutely necessary.]

Reb Mordechai originally came from Horodok, and had been sent to Czasznyk by the Mitteler Rebbe, who instructed the Czasznyk Chassidim to raise six paper rubles (two silver rubles) a month for Reb Mordechai's salary, and to appoint him dean of the Czasznyk Chassidim.

"Reb Mordechai *Mashpia* was so impressed with me," related Reb Shmuel Dov, "that he admitted me to his *cheder*, which was in a small space partitioned off from the sideroom of the Lubavitcher shul. I spent a year and nine months under Reb Mordechai's guidance."

Rashdam related that once, during his stay in Czasznyk, a great desire arose among the young scholars to make a pilgrimage to Lubavitch. But Reb Mordechai *Mashpia* dissuaded them, saying that because the Mitteler Rebbe had been denounced to the government — and in fact he had recently been in prison — it was not a good time to travel to Lubavitch. A few weeks later, however, the rumor spread that the Mitteler Rebbe was traveling to the holy resting place of his father, the Alter Rebbe, in Haditch, and would be passing through the towns of Zhlobin and Homel. Consequently, ten of the young folk decided to travel secretly to one of these villages.

One night during the month of Av, they departed Czasznyk in stealth, arriving in Zhlobin a week later. There, they found several hundred guests from throughout the vicinity, all of whom had come to see the Mitteler Rebbe. To their disappointment, they learned that the Rebbe was spending the night at an inn near Zhlobin, and would remain in town for only one day. Moreover, being exhausted from the journey, he would not lecture on *Chassidus*, nor would he receive visitors for *yechidus*.

"I had the good fortune," related Rashdam, "to find favor with Reb Meir Tzvi the butler. He permitted me to assist him in bringing water, and in other simple tasks."

That evening, Rashdam had the privilege of hearing the Rebbe *davening Maariv* in his room. Later, when the butler Reb Meir Tzvi brought the Rebbe a glass of coffee, Rashdam caught a glimpse of his holy face. He waited up the whole night hoping for another chance to see the Rebbe's face. At about three o'clock, the butler opened the windows of the Rebbe's room. At that very moment the Rebbe emerged, and — passing through the room where Rashdam stood — he fixed a penetrating glance upon him.

Paradoxically, he was petrified, and at the same time captivated, by this. He knew that the Rebbe would have to pass through that room on his way back, but he lacked the courage to remain in his place. In great panic, he hid himself behind the door.

After the *davening*, Reb Meir Tzvi informed him that the Rebbe had inquired who he was. He had replied that Rashdam was from Czasznyk, an apprentice of Reb Mordechai Horodoker. He thought it possible that the Rebbe might request that Rashdam be brought to his room. Hearing this, Rashdam grew very frightened, not knowing what to do. He was completely unable to think coherently, for his mind had gone blank. But G-d (blessed be He), gave him the good sense to say some *Tehillim*; once he began his *Tehillim*, rivers of tears began to flow from his eyes.

Later, when Reb Meir Tzvi informed him that the Rebbe had actually sent for him, he became very flustered. It was only with Reb Meir Tzvi's assistance that he managed to enter the Rebbe's holy chamber. Being completely overcome emotionally, all he could manage to say were the few words,

"Rebbe! I want to be a chassid," after which he began to weep.

The holy Rebbe replied, "*Chabad* demands intellectual activity, understanding, and concentration. If you work hard, you will become a chassid. May G-d (blessed be He), grant you long life." Reb Meir Tzvi cautioned him not to reveal to anyone that he had had the great privilege of going in to see the holy Rebbe.

During the day that the Mitteler Rebbe remained in Zhlobin, about two thousand chassidim arrived from the surrounding villages. Since it was Thursday, the chassidim made a great effort to influence the Rebbe to remain in Zhlobin for *Shabbos,* but to no avail. At two in the afternoon the Rebbe departed Zhlobin, after issuing an edict that no person — except those who were traveling in his official entourage — should dare attempt to follow him on the road.

After the Rebbe left, Rashdam went to seek his companions from Czasznyk, who were mingled among the great throng of people. With much effort he managed to find them, and with great regret at not having heard the Rebbe lecture on *Chassidus,* they returned to Czasznyk. On Monday, after Rashdam arrived home in Czasznyk, during a moment when no one else was present in the *beis hamedrash,* Reb Mordechai *Mashpia* said that he detected an aura of spiritual purity about him. Reb Mordechai commanded Rashdam to tell him what had happened to him, and he told him everything.

Rashdam married a Czasznyk woman — his cousin, the daughter of his maternal uncle. During the five years following his wedding, he was supported by his father-in-law, while he continued under the tutelage of Reb Mordechai *Mashpia.* In 5592 [1832], when the Rebbe the *Tzemach Tzedek* visited Minsk, Reb Mordechai *Mashpia* traveled there to see him, together with many of the young scholars. On that occasion, he took Rashdam along with him, and that was the first time he saw the holy *Tzemach Tzedek*.

In 5594, Rashdam made his first pilgrimage to Lubavitch, but for personal reasons he was unable to remain longer that two weeks. Various circumstances prevented him from making another trip to Lubavitch until Elul 5596, but this time he remained in Lubavitch until Nissan 5597. He was then about thirty years old, and he had already achieved fame among the chassidim. The Rebbe's holy sons gave him honor, and even the Rebbe the *Tzemach Tzedek* himself bestowed great favor upon him.

As the chassid Reb Chanoch Hendel tells, by the year 5603 [1843] Rashdam was considered one of the foremost chassidim.[8] When the Rebbe returned home to Lubavitch from his trip to Petersburg during that year, Rashdam occupied a place in the first rank of the elder chassidim who went forth to welcome him.

In my library of original manuscripts — which G-d in His great kindness has given me the privilege of possessing — there are numerous letters written by my saintly great-uncles, the *Tzemach Tzedek's* sons, to Rashdam.

I herewith enclose a copy of one of the letters my saintly grandfather — the holy Rebbe Maharash — sent to the chassidim of Borisov.[9] I have chosen this particular letter for several reasons. Besides the central theme dealing with the importance of business people setting aside time to study *Chassidus*, and the necessity of designating a specific person whose only task is to look after the spiritual needs of the

---

8. [He was only about 35 years old at that time.]
9. [A translation of this letter and the accompanying notes appears in Appendix A.]

chassidim, this letter gives a clear picture of the great stature of the chassid Rashdam.

Rashdam's life story comprises a long chain of Torah, *avodah*, and involvement in the spiritual welfare of chassidim. He fulfilled the instructions given to him by the Mitteler Rebbe, "*Chabad* demands intellectual activity, understanding, and concentration. If you work hard, you will become a chassid."

For His part, G-d (blessed be He), fulfilled the Mitteler Rebbe's blessing, and granted him long life. I don't know the exact dates, but I infer from all the stories that Rashdam was born about the year 5568 [1808] and passed away in 5649 [1889], having lived more than eighty years.

Rashdam left many manuscripts; some are transcriptions of chassidic discourses he heard from the *Tzemach Tzedek* and the Rebbe Maharash, and others are his own compositions, explanatory remarks, and longer commentaries presented in orderly fashion. More importantly, he left behind a whole generation of apprentices and students, many of whom occupy lofty positions among *Chabad* Chassidim. Thus, he earned for himself a memorial of everlasting fame and adoration.

REB CHAYIM YEHOSHUA[1]

BY
REB AVRAHAM ABBA PERSAN[2]

The famous chassid Reb Dov Zev of Yekaterinoslav related the following story:

While he was a *shadar* of the Rebbe Maharash, Reb Dov Zev regularly visited the city of Gluchov, where one of the elders of the chassidim, Reb Chayim Yehoshua, lived. Whenever Reb Dov Zev visited Gluchov, he delighted in listening to Reb Chayim Yehoshua tell stories of the chassidim of the old days.

When Reb Dov Zev arrived in Gluchov in the year 5637 [1877], Reb Chayim Yehoshua was already an old man of eighty-seven. He felt his end approaching, and so he sent for the elder chassidim of the city: Reb Avraham Zalman *HaKohen*, Reb Shlomo Menachem the *melamed*, and Reb Ephraim Fishel the *melamed*; he requested that they also invite the visiting *shadar*.

---

1. From *HaTamim*, Issue No. 6, pp. 97-99; 2 & 13 *Nissan* 5697; appears as a continuation of the story of Reb Gavriel *Nossai Chein*. We include some excerpts from the same issue, pp. 8-12, taken from the Previous Rebbe's remarks on a letter by the *Tzemach Tzedek* (see Appendix B).
2. [In *HaTamim*, the subtitle reads, "From stories told by Reb Avraham Abba Persan." It seems, however, that the article was actually written by the Previous Rebbe himself. Apparently the Previous Rebbe had heard the stories from Reb Avraham Abba, and recorded them in his diary. The editors of *HaTamim* included — as a footnote — a brief biography of Reb Avraham Abba; (a translation appears in a later chapter).]

Upon discovering that the chassid Reb Chayim Yehoshua was sick, the *gaon* Reb Dov Zev went to visit him. Reb Chayim Yehoshua's illness lasted for a month. Although his strength gradually ebbed, he remained in full possession of his mental faculties until the very end, and he told his visitors various stories. The following is his deathbed declaration, as he dictated it to them:

During the year 5593 or 5594 [1832, 33] I spent all eight days of Chanukah in Lubavitch with the Rebbe the *Tzemach Tzedek*. There, I heard three chassidic discourses, all based on the theme that the war against the Greeks was a spiritual battle. As the Sages teach us,[3] [the Greeks demanded of the Jews that they,] "Write upon the horn of an ox that you have nothing to do with the G-d of Israel." But through *mesirus nefesh* the Jews overcame them. The Rebbe spoke highly of the *avodah* of *mesirus nefesh* to sanctify G-d's Holy Name, as was performed by Rabbi Akiva and others like him.

At the time, I was a little over forty years old. I, my four brothers, and my two brothers-in-law, lived in a hamlet called Zastke, near Kalisk [in Vitebsk County of White Russia]. Our father Reb Avraham Yisrael — a chassid of the Alter Rebbe and of his son the Mitteler Rebbe — had originally settled there. He brought us up to study Torah and to be farmers. We also took great pains to observe the *mitzvah* of catering to guests.

One winter's night during the year 5595 or 5596, we suddenly heard a knocking at the door. Getting out of bed and opening the door, I saw two Jews wrapped in winter cloaks, covered with snow, standing in the doorway. I extended my hand in greeting, and invited them to take off their cloaks and sit near the stove to warm themselves. I also offered them glasses of tea, and bread with butter and whey.

---

3. [*Bereishis Rabbah* 16:4.]

While they sat down to eat, I went out to check the barn. Once outdoors, I heard what sounded like a child crying. I paid no attention to it, for I assumed it was a cat. But when I came closer to the source of the sound, I heard that it was the voice of a child.

"Who's that crying?" I called.

"It's I, Binyomin!" a trembling voice replied.

Following the sound of the voice, I approached the sleigh that the guests had parked at the edge of the courtyard. When I looked inside, my whole body began to quake. I saw two small boys lying there, bound up in chains: one was sleeping, the other crying.

In those days, there were many "snatchers" — men who would kidnap Jewish children, take them away, and sell them to other communities to be handed over to the military. Seeing the children, I immediately guessed that the men were snatchers, and that these were stolen children. I was afraid that they would also kidnap some of our own children.

I quickly removed the chains from the two boys, lifted them from the sleigh, and took them to the home of my brother Michael, out in the garden. My brother Michael had already woken from his sleep; I told him of my suspicions, and hurried home.

When I arrived home, I found one of the guests sitting next to my son Ephraim Zalman. I woke everyone in the house and whispered to them that these Jews were snatchers, and that they were carrying two boys bound in chains, who had undoubtedly been kidnapped.

The Jew seated near my son Ephraim Zalman said, "He looks like a good boy. G-d in Heaven has burdened me with two sons who are insane, and speak lies. I have no choice but to chain them up and take them to the psychiatrist in Vitebsk."

Meanwhile, my brother Michael gave the children food and drink, and locked them in a room. He then came to my house, and seeing the two Jews he became furious. He went over to them saying, "*Shalom Aleichem*, Jewish snatchers! Leave this house immediately, or you'll be sorry!"

The two Jews did not yet realize that they had been found out, and one said to the other, "Let's get out of here. As you can see, we've fallen in among heartless Jews who have no pity for an unfortunate person such as yourself, who is taking his insane sons to a psychiatrist.

"I myself," the Jew continued saying to us, "live in a small village, just like you. And when I found out that the tar maker who lives in the forest nearby had children who had gone incurably insane, I took pity on him. I harnessed my horse, and am now conveying him and his two sons to the psychiatrist in Vitebsk."

The Jews left my house in a huff. When they came to the sleigh and discovered that the children were gone, they immediately returned screaming. But they soon realized that screaming would do them no good, and they hurriedly fled the village, leaving the children behind with us.

A month later, it was my brother Michael's regular time to visit Lubavitch and see the Rebbe the *Tzemach Tzedek*. When he entered the Rebbe's room and told him about the children, the Rebbe's face beamed with joy. He gave us all his blessing, instructing us to keep the children for a year and then to take them home. The children remained with us and studied together with our own sons under the *melamed* Reb Yeruchem Zev, doing very well.

From that time on I had an overpowering desire to work at *pidyon sh'vuyim*. Unable to restrain myself, I went to the

Tzemach Tzedek and told him of this great desire. The Rebbe agreed, and prepared an itinerary for me to follow in this work. Three or four months a year — sometimes in the summer and sometimes in the winter — I would journey to various places, and ransom children who had been kidnapped and handed over to become "cantonists." I pursued this work for seven years, until I was finally caught and came within an inch of losing my life.

**[The story is now continued by
Reb Avraham Abba Persan]:**

The chassid Reb Chayim Yehoshua spent four months in the vicinity of Kazan. At home, his business affairs often took him to the small villages, and so he was quite familiar with the ways of village folk. He would travel from one small village to another, ransoming the children. Some of them fled on their own after they were released. As for the others, he had to care for them and find them a place of refuge.

Reb Chayim Yehoshua pursued his work in clever fashion. Upon first arriving in a village, he would purchase some products of that village: wool, linen, and the like. This gave the impression that his visit was for business purposes. Only incidentally would he inquire about the young boys of the vicinity.

One day, a Jew who spoke Yiddish with a Vohlynian accent arrived at the village where he was staying. He too had come to purchase the local products of wool and linen, and he became friendly with Reb Chayim Yehoshua. Reb Chayim Yehoshua innocently took him at face value, and they remained together for a month. But the newcomer spied on Reb Chayim Yehoshua, eventually discovering everything he was doing in ransoming the cantonists.

Reb Chayim Yehoshua had eight boys for whom he had not yet found homes. Some of them were living with him in Kazan, while others had gone to the townsfolk to beg for food. His friend the wool-and-linen merchant assisted him in ransoming the cantonists and in making further arrangements for them. With his help he managed to place six of the children in Kazan. Reb Chayim Yehoshua decided to take the remaining two home with him when he left.

On the very day that Reb Chayim Yehoshua was planning to depart, three armed soldiers suddenly appeared, in the company of the merchant from Vohlynia. They arrested the chassid Reb Chayim Yehoshua and bound him in chains. As soon as the children caught sight of the soldiers, they ran for their lives, and alarmed the children who had been placed in the city. All of them disappeared, and were never heard from again. During the next six months, Reb Chayim Yehoshua was moved from one jail to another, bound in chains, until he was finally brought to Vitebsk.

There, Reb Chayim Yehoshua was imprisoned under very harsh conditions. At first the governor wanted him tried for treason by a military court, and he boasted that he would execute Reb Chayim Yehoshua by hanging. It took a great deal of persuasion to influence him to hold the trial in civil court.[4]

Reb Chayim Yehoshua remained in the Vitebsk prison for three months before the governor finally released him. The *Tzemach Tzedek* lent him a sum of money with which to purchase goods and start a business. He advised him to settle in the city of Gluchov [Czernigov County of "Little Russia" (Ukraine)], and gave him his blessing. Reb Chayim Yehoshua lived in Gluchov for twenty-five years, and he

---

4. [Eventually, through the intercession of Reb Gavriel *Nossai Chein*, he was set free, as described in the following chapter.]

prospered financially. From time to time he would travel to Lubavitch to the Rebbe the *Tzemach Tzedek,* and after [the *Tzemach Tzedek*] passed away, to his son the Rebbe Maharash.

[Reb Chayim Yehoshua's deathbed declaration — quoted by Reb Dov Zev — continues]:

After my release, I again visited the Rebbe, who designated the city of Gluchov as my new home. He blessed me with long life, and added the promise, "You will be with me in my domain."[5] Today or tomorrow, I will return my soul to my Maker. My final request of you is that after my casket is covered with earth, a *minyan* of men should make the following declaration:

> Holy Rebbe, son-in-law of the [Mitteler] Rebbe, and grandson of the [Alter] Rebbe: your servant Chayim Yehoshua ben Esther has died; before his death, he appointed us his agents to do a *mitzvah* and inform you that your servant Chayim Yehoshua ben Esther has died, and to remind you of the promise you made to your servant Chayim Yehoshua ben Esther in reward for his labors in the *mitzvah* of *pidyon sh'vuyim* — the promise that, "You will be with me in my domain."

They all promised Reb Chayim Yehoshua that they would do as he asked. The next morning, after he *davened Shacharis* and put on *Rabbeinu Tam's tefillin,* he delivered up his soul with a clear mind, and while reciting *Shema Yisrael.* That same day, Reb Chayim Yehoshua was buried.

The chassid Reb Dov Zev continued relating the story: when the casket was covered with earth, ten of the men

---

5. [I.e., his place in *Gan Eden* would be close to that of the Rebbe.]

stood there and recited the message quoted above. When I later came to the Rebbe[6] in Lubavitch and repeated to him Reb Chayim Yehoshua's story and his final request, the Rebbe said:

> So may it be done on High! Divine service in actual deed elevates one to the highest levels. Reb Chayim Yehoshua was a clever chassid, and he provided himself with a wonderful place for his eternal home. My father is a man of his word, and he will surely keep his promise.

---

6. The Rebbe Maharash, son of the Rebbe the *Tzemach Tzedek*.

REB GAVRIEL *NOSSAI CHEIN*[1]

BY
REB AVRAHAM ABBA PERSAN[2]

Sometime during the last twenty years of the fifth century,[3] a certain Jewish family that originally stemmed from Prague emigrated from Poland and settled in the city of Vitebsk in White Russia. In those days, the use of family surnames was still unheard of among the Jews of that vicinity. Usually, individual Jews were named for some event that occurred in their lives, their trade or business, their physical appearance, or their place of origin. Since this family originally stemmed from Prague, they were known by the name "Prager."

The patriarch of the family, Reb Gavriel, was then between sixty and seventy years old, and he possessed an imposing appearance and pleasant disposition. His home was open to guests — especially Torah scholars — whom he would welcome with open arms.

Reb Gavriel had served as manager of the estates of a Polish count on the outskirts of one of the cities of Poland. This count happened to inherit an estate near Vitebsk from his uncle. He gave this estate as a gift to his younger son, who had recently married the daughter of the governor of Vitebsk. The old count asked Reb Gavriel to accompany his

---

1. From *HaTamim*, Issue No. 6, pp. 89-97; 2 & 13 Nissan 5697.
2. [See previous chapter, note 2.]
3. [The fifth century (of the sixth millenium) in the Jewish reckoning. The last twenty years of this century were 1721-1740.]

son, the young count, to Vitebsk, and manage his estate there.

Reb Gavriel replied that, although it would be difficult for him to move away from the place where he had been living for more than fifty years, he was nevertheless willing to fulfill the nobleman's request. However, he first wished to put the affairs of the count's local estate in order, and to find an honest person to serve as his replacement. The count thanked him, and told him that he desired Reb Gavriel's eldest son to succeed him.

Reb Gavriel had two sons, both of whom had families of their own. The elder son, Reb Shlomo Yaakov, was a businessman; the younger son, Reb Aharon Tzvi, still sat studying Torah, together with a few of his young contemporaries.

Reb Gavriel and his son Reb Shlomo Yaakov decided to accept the count's offer. Reb Shlomo Yaakov remained behind to manage the count's estates, while Reb Gavriel, his younger son Reb Aharon Tzvi, and their families, moved to Vitebsk. The houses in which they had lived were donated to three Torah scholars, to live in rent free.

When Reb Gavriel arrived in Vitebsk, the young count introduced him to his father-in-law, the governor, praising him greatly. The governor welcomed him warmly, and suggested that he find a place for himself and his family to live, in one of the four properties he owned in the city. Reb Gavriel thanked him for his kindness, but declared that it would be better for business if he at first lived on one of the estates of the son-in-law, the count.

After about a year had passed, Reb Gavriel moved his residence to Vitebsk itself, building a house and a *shul* in his courtyard. There, he maintained ten Torah scholars who were supported at his expense. These were ascetic and chaste individuals, who sat in his *beis hamedrash* studying Torah with diligence. Little-by-little, his son Reb Aharon Tzvi took over the management of the estates, while Reb Gavriel himself came only occasionally to inspect and oversee their management.

The heads of the Vitebsk community, seeing the esteem in which Reb Gavriel was held by the governor and his son-in-law (and thus, also by the other city and county officials), appointed him president of the congregation. Due to his good nature, Reb Gavriel treated everyone with kindness.

Sometime during the next ten years or so, his son Reb Aharon Tzvi married off his children to prestigious families of Vitebsk, and supported them with affluence. But he suffered a sudden loss, when his wife died in the cholera epidemic (may we be spared) during the summer of 5491 [1731]. When the required three festivals passed, Reb Aharon Tzvi married a second wife, who was the daughter of one of the elder scholars of Vitebsk — the *gaon* Reb Shlomo — and the widow of Reb Yoel *Masmid*.

Four years after his second marriage, his father Reb Gavriel passed away. He was remembered with honor, and the greatest Torah personalities eulogized him; he was also mourned by all the Jews of Vitebsk. About a year later, a son was born to Reb Aharon Tzvi, and he named him Gavriel after his father. The young Gavriel surpassed all his classmates with his diligent study and gentle conduct. His father gave him a good education, and he excelled at his studies.

When he reached the appropriate age, one of the aristocratic Jews of Vitebsk took him as a husband for his daughter. He stipulated that he was to sit and study Torah exclusively, while [the father-in-law] would provide for all his needs. Thus, the young scholar Reb Gavriel devoted himself to Torah and *avodah* for nine years, supported by his father-in-law.

At that time, the young genius Reb Schneur Zalman — who had been born in the village of Liozna, and was the son-in-law of the wealthy Reb Yehuda Leib Segal — achieved prominence among the scholars and *geonim* of Vitebsk. Many of the foremost young scholars, including Reb Gavriel, would refer to him their questions and difficulties in Scripture, *Mishnah, Gemara, Halachah,* and *Aggadah.* They were always delighted with his replies.

A few years later, Reb Gavriel's father-in-law passed away. To support his family, Reb Gavriel was now obliged to engage in business; he therefore took over the operation of a large store he had inherited from his father-in-law. But he continued to set aside time which he devoted to studying Torah. From time to time, he would visit the *gaon* Reb Schneur Zalman to enjoy his Torah discourses, together with several of his friends who were Torah scholars.

It was then that the Alter Rebbe, Reb Schneur Zalman, traveled to Mezritch. When he returned to Vitebsk, the city was in an uproar. The prominent citizens of Vitebsk, led by the elderly Reb Shlomo, insisted that his wealthy father-in-law Reb Yehuda Leib Segal evict him from his home, and that his daughter demand a divorce.

The Alter Rebbe notified the Rabbinical Court of Vitebsk that he was prepared to hold a debate about the practices of the Baal Shem Tov and his disciple the *Maggid* of Mezritch. He maintained that the proclamations and bans published against the Baal Shem Tov and his disciple the *Maggid* of Mezritch in the year 5517 [1757], were contrary to Torah law.

After lengthy discussion of the issue by members of the Rabbinical Court and other scholars of the city, it was decided to accept the proposal of "Reb Y. L. Segal's son-in-law" (that is how people who opposed the views of the Baal Shem Tov and the *Maggid* of Mezritch referred to the Alter Rebbe) and to hear what he would say. They declared that his Torah study had caused him to grow haughty.

A public debate — lasting a full week — was held, during which the Rebbe explained the views of the Baal Shem Tov, and of his own mentor the *Maggid* of Mezritch. Afterwards, a great dispute erupted among the leaders of Vitebsk: some of them had now become advocates [of the Alter Rebbe], while others remained opposed.

A substantial number of the young scholars, including Reb Gavriel, were inclined to follow the Alter Rebbe, and they scheduled fixed times when they would study together. The parents of these young scholars, their in-laws, and other relatives persecuted them at every opportunity for going to the Alter Rebbe to study the Baal Shem Tov's teachings. But they accomplished nothing by this, for the more they tormented them, the more firmly they clung to the chassidic ways.

The magnate Reb Aharon Tzvi, Reb Gavriel's father, was also an opponent of the Alter Rebbe, and more than once he requested the governor to expel Reb Y. L. Segal's son-in-law from the city. But since the time that the Rebbe had solved the two famous mysteries,[4] he was held in great esteem by the governor, and they could do nothing to him.

When the Alter Rebbe accepted the position as *Maggid* of Liozna, Reb Gavriel was among the first to make pilgrimages to him in Liozna. From that time on, his father, his brother, his brothers-in-law, and all his other relatives began to afflict him with all sorts of persecutions, making every effort to ruin him financially. But the chassid Reb Gavriel

---

4. The mystery of the sundial [*Sefer HaToldos, Admur HaZakein*, Vol. I, p. 84ff.], and the cure for sunstroke.

persisted in following his own way, paying no attention to anything his father, his brother, and their confederates — the opponents of the Rebbe — did to him.

Reb Gavriel continued visiting the Alter Rebbe in Liozna regularly. But never did he complain to the Rebbe about his financial problems, which grew worse from day to day because of the persecution by his relatives. He even contributed generous sums — as he had always done — to all the charity funds that the Alter Rebbe collected from the chassidim. This included charities for both public affairs (such as supporting the Rebbeim in the Holy Land, *pidyon sh'vuyim*, and the like) and for private individuals.

Reb Gavriel and his wife were greatly distressed by the fact that twenty-five years had already passed since their wedding, and they had no children. They also suffered from the torments of his mother, his sisters, and his sisters-in-law, who heaped the most awful curses upon his wife and himself.

The chassid Reb Gavriel, who had been trained by the first generation of the Alter Rebbe's chassidim, knew chassidic ways well, and he followed them with *mesirus nefesh*.

He refused to exploit what was holy for his personal use, and so he never complained to the Alter Rebbe about his material circumstances; not even about his condition of childlessness. Nevertheless, the One Who ordains all things caused events to evolve in such a way that Reb Gavriel received a threefold salvation: children, long life, and sustenance.

It once occurred that the Alter Rebbe was involved in *pidyon sh'vuyim*, and he assigned Reb Gavriel a substantial sum to be contributed toward this *mitzvah*. When Reb Gavriel told his wife about the assessment, she perceived that he was not too happy about it. Knowing how dedicated he was to the Alter Rebbe, and with what great joy he always obeyed his orders, she understood that something was bothering him this time, and she asked him to explain himself.

Reb Gavriel then revealed to her that — because of the persecution by their relatives — he was financially ruined, and could not raise the sum that the Alter Rebbe had assessed him.

To this, his wife replied, "Didn't you often tell me that the Rebbe always stresses in his teachings that one must believe and trust in G-d, and remain constantly joyful? So why are you distressed? Surely G-d will help, and we will be able to satisfy the assessment that the Alter Rebbe placed upon us."

Reb Gavriel's wife, Chanah Rivkah, was a chassidic woman. She went to pawn her pearls and some of her other jewelry. She brought the money to her husband, saying, "Now we have the sum that the Rebbe assessed us," and gave him a sealed packet. "Here is the entire amount," she said, and she advised him to go immediately to Liozna and put it in the Rebbe's holy hand.

Reb Gavriel replied that — under ordinary circumstances — when the Rebbe assessed chassidim for charitable donations, he would send his agent to collect the money that was due. Undoubtedly, he would do the same this time, and they ought to wait for the agent's arrival.

After some time passed, his brothers denounced him to the government, and caused him great monetary loss. Reb Gavriel was afraid that he might need the money for his own use, and would be unable to resist the temptation. Therefore, he took up the packet of money, and set out for Liozna.

When he came into the Rebbe's presence, he deposited the parcel of money on the table, explaining that he had managed to raise the sum the Rebbe had assessed him. But since his financial circumstances were not what they used to be, he feared that some unavoidable mishap might occur before the expected arrival of the agent. Therefore, he had brought the money in person, earlier.

When Reb Gavriel deposited the parcel of money in front of the Rebbe, the Rebbe instructed him to open the packet and count it. They examined the coins, and behold! The coins shone as brightly as if they had just been newly minted.

Reb Gavriel was quite perplexed, and could think of no explanation for this phenomenon. The Alter Rebbe leaned upon his elbows [in *deveikus*] for quite some time; then, he raised his holy head and said:

"Among the items donated for building the *Mishkan*, were gold, silver, and copper. But there was nothing that shone with such brilliance as the copper mirrors, brought by the women, from which the wash-stand and its base were cast.[5] Now the wash-stand and its base were the last to be made among all the utensils of the *Mishkan*. But they were the first to be used, before all other forms of sacrificial worship in the *Mishkan*.

"Tell me," asked the Alter Rebbe, "Where did you get this money?"

Reb Gavriel then related to the Alter Rebbe that for more than ten years his father, brothers, and other relatives had persecuted him and ruined him financially. But he had refused to pay any attention to that.

After being notified of the assessment, he had told his wife that he lacked the means to pay such a sum. Thereupon, his wife — Chanah Rivkah bas Beila — had gone and pawned some of her jewelry and precious stones without his

---

5. [See Appendix C, for a chassidic discourse on the subject of "shining".]

knowledge. She had then given him this packet, informing him that it contained the required sum of money, and requesting that he go immediately and deliver it to the Rebbe.

He himself had wished to await the arrival of the Rebbe's agent. But meanwhile he had found himself in the position of having been denounced. People who knew about such matters had predicted that he would have to pay a heavy fine, and therefore he was very afraid that the money would be gone. For this reason, he had hurried to deliver it to the Rebbe.

The Rebbe leaned upon his elbows [in *deveikus*] for quite some time; then, he raised his holy head and said:

> "A woman of judgment has annulled the judgment."[6] May G-d grant — to you and to your wife — sons and daughters, and long life, so that you may see your descendants for several generations. May G-d grant you — time and again — success in all your undertakings, and great wealth. May you find favor in the eyes of everyone you meet. Close your shop, and open a business in jewelry and precious stones instead.

Reb Gavriel returned home in joyful spirits, repeating to his wife everything the Rebbe had said, and the blessings he had conferred upon him. He then asked her about the coins that shined and sparkled.

"I polished them with sand until they were mirror-like and sparkled like the stars of heaven," replied his wife. "I did this so that G-d (blessed be He) and the holy Rebbe,

---

6. [A play on words. The quote cited by the Alter Rebbe in its Aramaic original (*Sanhedrin* 95a), states "Delaying the judgment overnight annuls the judgment." The Aramaic word for "overnight delay" (בת) is the same as the Hebrew word for "daughter" (or "woman").]

would elevate our status. Then, our fortune would begin to sparkle and shine, while our enemies would be humiliated."

Reb Gavriel closed his shop and began dealing in precious stones. G-d granted him success in this enterprise, and he found favor in the eyes of the noblemen who owned the estates surrounding Vitebsk. They were among his steady customers, and his reputation became known even among the government ministers.

His business grew and prospered from day to day, while the allegations against him were utterly forgotten. A year later, his wife gave birth to their first son, whom they named Chayim.

Within three years, the chassid Reb Gavriel grew extremely wealthy, for he was successful in everything he undertook. He found favor in the eyes of everyone he met, and so earned the name Reb Gavriel *Nossai Chein*.[7]

Reb Gavriel carried on with his business for over forty years. He married off his sons and daughters to prominent families of the city of Shklov. Afterwards, he gave the business over to his sons, devoting all his time to Torah and *avodah*, and to charitable works. His home was open to visitors, and due to his efforts the chassidic community of Vitebsk grew and prospered.

When the chassid Reb Chayim Yehoshua[8] was arrested and brought to Vitebsk in chains, the elderly Reb Gavriel was away in Shklov attending the wedding of his youngest son's grandson. He remained away from home for several months. By the time he returned to Vitebsk, the city's governor had already been persuaded to hold Reb Chayim Yehoshua's trial in the civil court.

---

7. ["Who Finds Favor."]
8. [The story of Reb Chayim Yehoshua appeared in the previous chapter.]

Since the elderly Reb Gavriel was held in high esteem by the governor,[9] he went to him to speak in Reb Chayim Yehoshua's defense. He again found favor in the governor's eyes, and his request was fulfilled; Reb Chayim Yehoshua was set free, with the stipulation that he must leave the vicinity of Vitebsk, and that no one must know of it.

Reb Gavriel *Nossai Chein* passed away in the year 5606 [1846] at the ripe old age of a hundred and ten years. He was eulogized by the *gaon* Reb Aizik,[10] who cried, "Woe, a chassid is gone! Woe, a master of humility is gone!" Two years later, his wife — the chassidic matron Chanah Rivkah — also died. May their souls be bound up in the parcel of eternal life.

---

9. [When the Mitteler Rebbe was denounced to the government and brought to Vitebsk, Reb Gavriel managed to persuade the governor to ease the conditions of his imprisonment. Instead of confining him in the common jail, he was held under guard in a private home.]

10. For more information about the *gaon* Reb Aizik of Vitebsk, see Issue No. 4 of *HaTamim*, "Fathers of *Chassidus*," section 22.

THE VILENKER BROTHERS[1]

BY
REB AVRAHAM ABBA PERSAN
(COMPILED FROM
THE PREVIOUS REBBE'S DIARY AND LETTERS)[2]

The chassidic Vilenkes[3] brothers — Reb Moshe and Reb Zev Volf — were descendants of a prominent family in Vilna. When the Alter Rebbe made his third or fourth trip to Vilna, in the year 5541 [1781], the chassidic *gaon* and master of wisdom, Reb Moshe [Vilenker], was already a young scholar with outstanding abilities. He told the Rebbe all the conceptual difficulties that had perplexed him during his studies. When the Rebbe answered each of his questions in order, the young scholar became a follower of the Rebbe.

Two months after the Alter Rebbe's departure from Vilna, the young scholar left home in secret. He traveled on foot to the Alter Rebbe in the city of Liozna. When he arrived, the Rebbe assigned him a place among the students of the first *cheder*,[4] because of his outstanding abilities.

When the Rebbe discovered that Reb Moshe had left home in secret, without his wife's permission, he refused to allow him to continue studying in Liozna. He insisted that

---

1. From *HaTamim*, issue No. 6, pp. 92-94. Appeared as part of the story of Reb Gavriel *Nossai Chein*, and the Previous Rebbe's remarks to the accompanying letter, pp. 8-12. The letter and the notes themselves are translated in Appendix B.
2. [See article on Reb Chayim Yehoshua, note 2. Note that R. Avraham Abba is occasionally referred to in the third person in this article.]
3. [The names "Vilenker," "Vilenkin," and "Vilenkes" are used interchangeably.]
4. See Issue No. 2 of *HaTamim*, "Fathers of *Chassidus*," section 12.

Reb Moshe first return home and obtain his wife's consent, as required by law.[5] Reb Moshe begged the Rebbe to allow him to remain for half a year, and the Rebbe acceded to this request.

More details of Reb Moshe's biography are written in my diary for the year 5659 [1899], as I heard them from the elderly chassid Reb Aharon of Dubravna.

The chassid Reb Zev Volf [Vilenker] was ten years old when his brother Reb Moshe suddenly disappeared. Though he returned a half year later, he remained for only two weeks. He took his wife and his two sons, and moved away from Vilna. His excuse was that G-d had sent him a business opportunity in the vicinity of Vitebsk.

The chassid Reb Zev Volf told his granddaughter's husband, the chassid Reb Avraham Abba Persan:

"For the next fifteen years, I had no idea what had happened to my brother Reb Moshe. But one day I discovered that my brother was among those who had the unique privilege of being disciples of the *Maggid* of Liozna. Having lived all my life among *misnagdim*, this news caused me great anguish during the next two or three years.

"When the Alter Rebbe was arrested and taken to the Imperial Capital, my friends all celebrated it as a holiday. I myself was saddened by this event, for I had heard of my brother Moshe's broad knowledge of the Torah, his fear of Heaven, and the praises heaped upon him by the Torah giants of Vilna. And so, when he chose the *Maggid* of Liozna as his Rebbe, I was convinced that the Rebbe must be a very great person.

---

5. [See *Kesuvos* 61b, 62b.]

"After the Rebbe's release from prison, the chassidic community of Vilna grew in strength, and I visited them from time to time. I made my first trip to the Alter Rebbe after he settled in Liadi, and I remained there for nine months. It was there that I was reunited with my brother Reb Moshe, after a twenty-year separation."

The chassid Reb Moshe was cherished by the Rebbe the *Tzemach Tzedek*. He was very dear to him, for he repeated to him the Torah discourses he had heard from the Alter Rebbe when he first arrived in Liozna. Because of this, the *Tzemach Tzedek* acceded to Reb Moshe's request and studied with his brother Reb Zev Volf twice a week, reviewing with him and explaining the chassidic discourses delivered by the Rebbe each *Shabbos*. According to a story told by the chassid Reb Avraham Abba Persan during the summer of 5652 [1892], the *Tzemach Tzedek* was about sixteen years old at the time, while Reb Zev Volf was about thirty.

The following is a story that Reb Avraham Abba Persan quoted from his "father-in-law's father-in-law", illustrating the love with which chassidim bore their suffering:

One day, I was walking along an alley in the poor people's neighborhood of Vilna. It was my habit to visit them occasionally, to fulfill the *mitzvah* of giving charity anonymously.

As I passed a house whose windows were very low, reaching to the ground, I heard the sound of joyful singing. I assumed that they must be celebrating a *bris milah* or a wedding, and so I entered to partake of the feast held in celebration of the *mitzvah*.

Upon entering, I saw about twenty people sitting crowded together, for the room was very small. On the table lay a loaf of black bread, a bottle of whiskey, and some small cups.

Most of the participants were dressed in tatters, their faces lean and emaciated. Nevertheless, they sang with such joyful voices that I was greatly impressed.

Among the participants sat a tall, thin man, whose face was barely visible. His head and most of his body were wrapped in a towel. From time to time, a sigh escaped his lips, apparently from his painful injuries. Nevertheless, his joy was greater than that of the other participants. I sat near the door and turned to the person sitting next to me, asking, "Is this repast being held in celebration of a *mitzvah*?"

"Yes," replied the man, "it's a feast in honor of a *mitzvah*."

"Who is the host of this repast?" I persisted in asking.

"That man, seated at the end of the table," he replied, pointing with his finger at the man wrapped in the towel.

When they finished singing, they began to wish each other *LeChayim!* At that point, I realized that the whole assembly consisted of members of "the cult." I was aware that my brother Reb Moshe had become a fervent chassid, fiercely attached to his Rebbe. Deep in my heart I held my brother Reb Moshe in great esteem, and so I was glad of the opportunity to observe the cult in person.

They offered me a glass, which I took, and recited *Shehakol*. Then, not knowing the exact cause for the celebration, I simply declared aloud, "*Mazel Tov* to the host of this celebration, *Mazel Tov* to everyone present!"

"Blessings upon you!" replied the host and everyone present, as they continued their singing.

When they finished the song, I stated that I too wished to have a share in the feast, by contributing a few pennies toward the purchase of some sweets or salads. But they refused to accept my offer, saying that if they did so they would lose a good thing.

The Vilenker Brothers

"What sort of good thing could you lose by eating some salad or sweets at a feast held in honor of a *mitzvah*?" I inquired.

"The only genuinely good thing, the plain bread and all the blessings that go with it," replied one of those present. He then resumed singing, and was joined by the others.

I remained at the gathering for two hours, and heard some teachings that they repeated in the name of their Rebbe and mentor.

Finally, I also learned the reason for the celebration: The man wrapped in the towel — whose name was Reb Shimon Chayim — was a relative of the famous Reb Meir Raphael's.[6] He had been an outstanding young scholar, and a disciple of Reb Eliyahu, the *Gaon* of Vilna.

A few years earlier, he had joined the cult and become a chassid, assembling groups of people and teaching them *Chassidus*. Two days earlier, a gang of young scholars of the *misnagdim* had seized him and brutally beaten him. This feast was being held to celebrate his great privilege in being beaten on account of *Chassidus*.[7]

The joy that chassidim felt because of their suffering on account of *Chassidus*, and the love and brotherhood that prevailed among members of the chassidic circle of Vilna, gave me no rest. Little by little I became attracted to them, until finally, I myself became one of their younger members.

---

6. [A prominent citizen of Vilna, and the chief benefactor of the congregation.]
7. [Another story illustrating the same point appears in the biography of Reb Avraham Abba Persan, in the next chapter.]

REB AVRAHAM ABBA PERSAN[1]

**BY
THE EDITORS OF *HATAMIM***

Reb Avraham Abba Persan was born in the village of Kreslavka, in Vitebsk County. His father was a close follower of the Mitteler Rebbe, and later of the *Tzemach Tzedek*. He was one of the most prestigious and wealthy chassidim in the entire Denenburg vicinity, and he had his son educated by *melamdim* who were elder chassidim in his hometown of Kreslavka, and in other villages near Denenburg and Polotzk.

Reb Avraham Abba was very diligent in his studies, and by nature he liked to have everything in precise order. His teachers trained him to memorize *Tanach*, the six orders of *Mishnayos*, and *Tanya*, and he could repeat them with remarkable exactness, perfectly to the letter.

He possessed strong emotions but a kind disposition nevertheless. His speech and his stride were slow and deliberate, and one can justifiably say that he measured his ways.[2] He loved his fellow man, and treated each person with kindness and respect.

From his early youth he displayed an interest in stories of the chassidim. He collected them as enthusiastically as other people collect jewels, and he would repeat these stories with infinite precision. While doing so he would add long

---

1. From *HaTamim*, Issue No. 6, pp. 89, 90. Appears as a footnote to the story of Reb Gavriel *Nossai Chein*, though we have taken several paragraphs from the story itself.
2. [Cf. *Rambam, Mishneh Torah, Hilchos De'os* 1:4.]

preambles, with details about the time and place that he first heard the stories, and the personalities of the people from whom he heard them.

He married a granddaughter of the famous chassid Reb Zev Volf (whose soul is in *Gan Eden*) — known among *Chabad* Chassidim as Reb Velvel Vilenker[3] — one of the foremost chassidim of the Alter Rebbe (author of the *Tanya* and *Shulchan Aruch*). After his marriage, the gates to the treasury of chassidic stories were opened to him.

It was an unbreakable rule with Reb Zev Volf that every *Shabbos* (in summertime, during the third meal of *Shabbos*; in wintertime, on *motzoei Shabbos*) he would gather together the elder chassidim of the city of Vitebsk. They would come to his home and discuss subjects of interest to chassidim, primarily stories about the holy Rebbeim.

Each related a story that he had seen himself, or repeated one that he had heard from older chassidim. Whenever Reb Avraham Abba Persan reminisced about these gatherings in the home of his father-in-law's father-in-law,[4] his face would light up with indescribable ecstasy.

Reb Avraham Abba Persan often said, "Whenever I recall the hours that elder chassidim spent *farbrenging* during my youth — especially *farbrengens* by the elder chassidim of the Alter Rebbe's generation, in the home of my father-in-law's father-in-law in Vitebsk — the memory banishes all pain and anguish from my heart, and infuses me with fresh spirit. It was a favorite expression of 'my elders' (that is how Reb Avraham Abba Persan referred to older chassidim) that a chassidic *farbrengen* is the outer courtyard of the *Beis HaMikdash* of *Chassidus*. Through it one may enter the inner

---

3. [The biography of the Vilenker Brothers appeared in the previous chapter.]
4. [I.e., Reb Zev Vilenker.]

courtyard, and from there one may enter the Most Holy Chamber."[5]

Reb Avraham Abba Persan related that a spirit of holiness hovered over the elder chassidim during the *farbrengens*. When any of them spoke, you could see — reflected in his face — the radiance of the subject he was discussing. This radiance penetrated deeply into the listener's soul, and the memory of it never faded.

Reb Avraham Abba Persan exhibited infinite patience when reciting *Tanya*, the six orders of *Mishnah*, the five books of *Chumash*, or *Tanach*, from memory, which he did with letter-perfect precision. He would manifest the same degree of patience and perfection whenever he read one of the holy epistles sent by the Rebbeim.

He would add explanations and commentary, and he told many tales about the significance of each nuance. Each story was punctuated and annotated, and he supplied the most minute details about the exact names and nicknames of each person mentioned. Each time he retold a story, he did so with the same patience and precision.

[The Rebbe Rayatz writes]:

"Whenever I heard a story from this precise chassid Reb Avraham Abba, I experienced the overpowering sensation that I was living in the time and place [of the story]. I could picture the scene in my imagination, as if the story were passing before my very eyes."

According to Reb Avraham Abba, the early chassidim would not trouble the Rebbe with their material problems — even when an extremely urgent matter was involved —

---

5. [Cf. Supra pp. 54-59.]

because their whole commitment was to truth, and not for personal gain.

A favorite quotation of the early chassidim was:

> The Israelites believed in Moshe *Rabbeinu* not because of the wondrous deeds he did (for when someone believes because of wondrous deeds, he still entertains some doubts). So why did they believe in him? Because they stood before Mt. Sinai, when our own eyes (not someone else's) witnessed, and our own ears (not someone else's) heard the fire, thunder, and lightning."
>
> *Rambam, Mishneh Torah, Hilchos Yesodei HaTorah,* 8:1.

The chassidim saw with their own eyes and heard with their own ears, the fire, thunder, and lightning when the Alter Rebbe delivered his Torah lectures.

It was because of this that they adhered to the Alter Rebbe, connecting their own souls with his holy and sublime soul. The chassidim, who suffered physically solely because they were chassidim, accepted their agony not only with love, but also with great joy; it was dearer to them than sacrificial offerings.

The chassid Reb Avraham Abba Persan heard from his father-in-law's father-in-law that the joy the chassidim in Vilna felt over their physical suffering, and their *mesirus nefesh* for *Chassidus*, were what had convinced him to become a chassid.

For example: in the city of Ulla [County of Vilna] there lived a young man named Reb Avraham Dov, who was related to the Torah scholar and chassid Reb Tzvi Hirsh. From his early youth he had been educated in the *yeshivos* of the *misnagdim*, and he was a young genius with great abilities. He was also a superb orator. When he first arrived in

Ulla, numerous chassidim already lived there. He gradually became attracted to them, eventually becoming a fervent chassid himself.

A few years later, he happened to meet several of his former *yeshivah* classmates in the city of Szventzian [County of Vilna]. Reb Avraham Dov spoke to them very highly of the chassidim, and taught them some chassidic teachings. Upon discovering that their former classmate had become a chassid, they became infuriated, and attacked him physically. With the assistance of a few additional young *misnagdim*, they beat him until they wounded him and broke his nose. From then on, he became known among the Ulla chassidim as "Reb Avraham Dov with the Big Nose."

On his deathbed, he declared: "For fifty years I was a faithful servant of the Alter Rebbe and his holy son the Mitteler Rebbe, and I occupied myself with studying their teachings. But my *avodah* has not made me feel the least bit superior. The only merit I possess is the great privilege I had, being beaten on account of *Chassidus*."

He then requested of all his friends that whenever they mentioned his name, they should add the nickname "With the Big Nose," for this was the merit he was taking with him, to serve him on the long journey he was about to make. When his friends promised to fulfill this request, he returned his soul to his Maker with complete serenity.[6]

When the number of years that his father-in-law had undertaken to support him expired, Reb Avraham Abba Persan settled in the city of Denenburg, where he lived for several years. Later, he moved to Vitebsk, where he lived until the year 5639 [1879]; after that he lived in Moscow, until the Jews were expelled from that city in the year 5652 [1892]. He then moved to Warsaw, where he remained for

---

6. [Another story illustrating this point appeared in the previous chapter.]

two years. In 5655 he finally settled in Königsberg, where he remained to the end of his days.

Typical Chassidic Businessmen: Reb Michael Aharon Pisarevsky and Reb Leib Posen[1]

BY
REB MEIR MORDECHAI CZERNIN[2]

The chassid Reb Michael Aharon Pisarevsky was a businessman of average income. He never had to do without the necessities of life, though at times his profits were abundant, and at other times, meager. He managed to marry off his sons and daughters, and to support them in the style customary for men of affairs.

There was nothing unique about his knowledge of the revealed Torah and *Chassidus*. He participated in the regularly-scheduled study sessions and public lectures, and also had a regular study session in private. His personality, however, was another matter. He was a very spirited individual with a "chassidic heart," always concerned with the welfare of others.

One of Reb Michael Aharon's acquaintances was the chassid Reb Nachman Lipa Zeltzer, a storekeeper who was well versed in the revealed Torah and in *Chassidus*. He taught classes in *Mishnayos* and in *Likkutei Torah* at the *shul*, and on *Shabbos* he spent a long time praying in the chassidic style. But he had a large family, including sons and daugh-

---

1. From *HaTamim*, Issue No. 7, pp. 102-108; 12-13 Tammuz 5697.
2. [The subtitle reads, "From stories told by Reb Meir Mordechai Czernin." The editors of *HaTamim* included — as a footnote — a brief biography of Reb Meir Mordechai (a translation appears in the next chapter).]

ters of marriageable age, and at that time his financial circumstances were extremely poor.

The chassid Reb Leib Posen owned a large store in Vitebsk. He had an abundant income and was a highly successful businessman. He owned several mansions, and was known as a magnate who supported his family with affluence. Though not a particularly friendly person, he gave charity generously and did other acts of kindness. People said of him that he gave away the required one tenth of his earnings, and his home was open to chassidim and other men of good deeds.

He had only a modest knowledge of the revealed Torah and *Chassidus*, but he was nevertheless deferential to Torah scholars. He participated in Torah study sessions, though he was unable to comprehend them adequately.

One of Reb Leib's acquaintances was the chassid Reb Shmuel Brin. Because of his outstanding abilities and his proficiency in the revealed Torah and *Chassidus*, Reb Shmuel was one of the foremost chassidim of Vitebsk. He was also famous for his shrewd manner of speech, his clever mind, and his understanding of business and commerce.

Though his business — general contracting — occupied much of his time, he nevertheless kept up a regular study session every day. His main subject was an in-depth study of *Gemara* and *Choshen Mishpat*; he also studied *Chassidus* in great depth. His success in business varied: sometimes up, and sometimes down. But he never paid attention to such trivial matters.

During the year 5640 [1880], strife and contention arose between the noblemen who owned the estates and the forests in the counties of Vitebsk and Paskov, and the local peasants [who worked for them]. As a result, the latter went on strike, and the cutting and transportation of wood ceased.

This was disastrous for Reb Shmuel Brin's business. At the same time, he was also swindled by some unscrupulous merchants. In the end, he lost his entire fortune, and was left seriously in debt.

Just before Pesach, our two chassidim — Reb Michael Aharon Pisarevsky and Reb Leib Posen — happened to be in Lubavitch at the same time, having come to spend *Shabbos* with the Rebbe Maharash.

When Reb Michael Aharon went in to the Rebbe for *yechidus*, the first subject he mentioned was his friend Reb Nachman Lipa Zeltzer. He described his poor financial situation, and the fact that his sons and daughters were of marriageable age. He discussed this at length, and begged for mercy in his behalf. The Rebbe gave his blessing that G-d would help him, and would exchange his situation of poverty for wealth. Reb Michael Aharon begged the Rebbe to guarantee that his blessing was a firm commitment.

Afterward, Reb Michael Aharon began to discuss his own situation. As he described his business dealings, it became apparent to the Rebbe that his business was in a sad state, and that he was impoverished and in debt. "If that's how things are," said the Rebbe, "then it seems that you're even worse off than Reb Nachman Lipa."

"Well, about myself, I know that I don't deserve anything better," said Reb Michael Aharon. "Therefore, it is forbidden to complain about my situation, and I will have to be satisfied with what I have."

The Rebbe covered his holy eyes with his hands and meditated for a short while. Then he said, "'If one prays for his fellow Jew, his own prayers are answered first.'[3] May G-d (blessed be He), grant you success."

---

3. [*Bava Kamma* 92a.]

"What do you think happened next?" said Reb Michael Aharon to Reb Meir Mordechai Czernin. "Why, Nachman Lipa suddenly became a success! Avraham Shalom the linen merchant suggested to him that — besides his store — he should trade in linens on the side. Reb Avraham Shalom's expertise in the linen business is legendary, and within half a year Reb Nachman Lipa became very wealthy.

"I myself also began to reap unusually large profits, both in my regular business, and on the side. Even when I casually mentioned to Chayim Yonah Ginsburg that it would be a good idea if he married off his daughter to Yaakov Leib Hurevitch, they both embraced my suggestion. They paid me a generous *shadchonus*, which was completely unexpected. At year's end — with the Rebbe's consent and according to his instructions — I purchased two mansions across the river, along with surrounding estates."

On the other hand, when Reb Leib Posen went in for *yechidus*, he began by discussing his own affairs at great length and in full detail. His entire oratory was devoted to a description of his financial status, and his request for a blessing. However, after he finished discussing his own situation, he sighed and added that Reb Shmuel Brin's affairs were in a very bad state.

"I certainly don't question the judgment of G-d (blessed be He)," said Reb Leib, "for whatever He does is undoubtedly the way things ought to be. Nevertheless, Reb Shmuel deserves great pity." The Rebbe covered his holy eyes with his hands and meditated deeply, but made no reply.

After Pesach, a fire broke out (may such a disaster not befall us) in the street where the warehouses containing Reb Leib Posen's linen were located. Everything was destroyed, resulting in a loss of several tens of thousands of rubles. At the same time, another fire broke out in his property across the river. His store burned down, along with all his merchandise, worth twenty thousand rubles. None of the damage was insured.

A few days later, he traveled to Lubavitch to see the Rebbe and tell him of the two disasters. Upon entering the Rebbe's chamber, he began to weep with great bitterness, saying that the two fires had cost him fifty thousand rubles. He then poured out his heart in bitter lament.

The Rebbe fixed a stern glance on him, and then said, "When you described Reb Shmuel Brin's poor situation — the loss of his entire fortune and his large debts — you took comfort in the fact that Heaven acts with justice. But when your own living and your own store are at stake, you raise a furor and cry; you don't even take comfort in the two mansions that you still own, nor in the sums that you have invested in businesses and in government securities. It seems that your standards regarding other people and those regarding yourself are totally different."

When Reb Leib emerged from the *yechidus*, he meditated deeply about the Rebbe's holy words. He realized that this evil had befallen him because of the sinful way in which he had spoken about Reb Shmuel's situation. For two days he remained in a state of severe confusion, at a loss for what to do about it. He finally decided to go in for a second *yechidus*, and to request that the Rebbe give him a penance. Upon entering the Rebbe's room, he was at first emotionally overcome, and unable to utter a word. When he calmed down a bit, he requested a program of *teshuvah* and atonement, promising that from then on he would concern himself with the welfare of others.

The Rebbe replied:

There is a tradition handed down from the Baal Shem Tov[4] that whenever someone pronounces judgment upon his fellow Jew — be it for good or for evil — he in fact pronounces judgment upon himself.

For example: if one says, "In reward for this good deed that so-and-so did, or that good thing that he said, he deserves to be helped by G-d with all his needs"; or, if one says, "As punishment for this wicked deed that so-and-so did, or those wicked words that he spoke, he deserves such-and-such"; whenever one speaks such words, he is in fact pronouncing his own judgment, whether for evil or for good.

Whenever someone justifies a Heavenly decree against another person, and does not feel anguish about it or pray for mercy in his behalf, by his own speech he pleads against his own cause. As a result, the Heavenly Court examines his conduct and his speech. But if one empathizes with his fellow Jew's anguish and prays for mercy in his behalf, he is rewarded.

Commenting on the Talmudic statement,[3] "If one prays for his fellow Jew, his own prayers are answered first," the Mitteler Rebbe quoted the Alter Rebbe: "If he himself is in need of something, he is answered first. And even if at the time he needs nothing, he nevertheless will receive his reward; he benefits first, for Heaven will reward him for his noble gesture."

---

4. [*Kesser Shem Tov,* Addendum, chs. 88, 89 and sources cited there; *In the Paths of Our Fathers,* p. 98.]

"And now," concluded the Rebbe, "you must give to Reb Shmuel Brin a personal loan of three thousand rubles interest-free, so that he may purchase merchandise and float it down to Riga by raft. Give it to him generously and cheerfully, thanking G-d that you have the privilege of doing good and charitable deeds. As for your own situation: travel to Moscow and buy goods for your store. May G-d replace your loss two-fold."

On the very day he returned home, he went to Reb Shmuel Brin, bringing a purse containing the money, as instructed. But he did not find him at home. Members of the household told him that Reb Shmuel had left two weeks earlier to inspect a convoy of rafts that were about to be floated down to Riga, and he had not yet returned.

A day passed by, then a second and a third day, and finally more than a week. But Reb Shmuel had not yet returned.

Reb Leib Posen waited impatiently day after day for Reb Shmuel's return, so that he could carry out the Rebbe's orders and give him the required loan. Each day seemed like a whole year, for he was anxious to make his own trip to Moscow and obtain merchandise for his own store.

Reb Leib was afraid to do things in a different order from the way the Rebbe had instructed him. The Rebbe had said that he should first make the loan to Reb Shmuel Brin so that he could purchase rafts and float them down to Riga; only then should he travel to Moscow and obtain goods for his store.

When Reb Leib arrived in *shul* for *Kabbalas Shabbos*, he saw Reb Shmuel Brin in the midst of a large crowd of people who were standing on the floor and on the benches. He had a joyful expression on his face, and appeared to be in a very cheerful mood as he spoke, while all the others listened.

At that moment, Reb Leib felt a twinge of envy: "Fortunate is a man with such a lot. More than two months have passed since his fortune was overturned and he became destitute, but he nevertheless manages to ignore it all. At this very moment he appears as though he were the luckiest person in the world!"

Reb Leib was startled out of his contemplation when Reb Hirsh Hirshman, the *gabbai*, banged on the table and cried out, "*Sha! Sha!* Reb Shmuel Brin is about to repeat the chassidic discourse that he heard from the Rebbe (may he be well) in Lubavitch."

As Reb Shmuel began to recite,[5] "My dove is in the crevices of the rock, hidden within the terraces" the *shul* suddenly became silent and all the listeners appeared exceedingly pleased.

That *Shabbos*, everyone in *shul* went to Reb Shmuel's home for *Kiddush*, where he repeated the discourse again. After *Minchah*, chassidim from the other *shuls* came, and Reb Shmuel repeated the discourse a third time. The joy of the chassidim knew no bounds.

After *Shabbos* was over, Reb Leib fought a battle with his own conscience: some say that at the conclusion of *Shabbos* or *Yom Tov* it is not appropriate to spend money, even for household needs; it is even less proper to spend it on someone who is not even a member of the household. He was unable to decide, when suddenly there appeared to him a vision of the Holy of Holies — a likeness of the Rebbe — standing before him and regarding him with a stern glance. Immediately, he took the purse with the three thousand rubles and went to Reb Shmuel Brin's home.

---

5. [*Shir HaShirim* 2:14. This verse introduces the chassidic discourse; possibly the first discourse of the *Hemshech Yonasi*, 5640.]

When he arrived, he discovered Reb Shmuel studying *Tur, Choshen Mishpat*. Reb Shmuel greeted him warmly, and began to speak words of encouragement concerning his recent losses in the fires (at the time, Reb Shmuel had been out of town). He reminded him of the well-known saying,[6] "after a fire, people become rich."

Reb Leib listened, and was amazed at Reb Shmuel's mental fortitude and inner strength, at a time when his fortunes were overturned (may G-d preserve us). Nine months earlier, he had been planning to purchase a large mansion, and now his fortune was at its lowest ebb; he had lost everything and now found himself in debt, unable to afford even a proper meal.

In spite of all the forgoing, he had gone to attend to the rafting business, had traveled to Lubavitch, returned with a chassidic discourse, and repeated it for the public benefit, happily and with a joyful voice. Now, he found him studying *Choshen Mishpat*, and what's more, Reb Shmuel was even attempting to comfort *him*!

"What do you plan to do now?" Reb Leib asked Reb Shmuel.

"As for myself," replied Reb Shmuel, "you know what women say: 'At the beginning of the week one must speak only of happy things'; my present situation is not fit to discuss at this moment. However, I am sincerely hopeful that G-d will help. I have done what I could: I went to inspect the ready-made rafts, and I also examined much good merchandise that was sitting on the river bank waiting to be loaded onto rafts. Now, it's up to G-d (blessed be He), to provide me with the necessary funds, and to grant me His abundant blessing."

---

6. *[Igros Kodesh, Admur HaZakein,* p. 189.]

[Reb Shmuel described his trip to Lubavitch]:

When I arrived in Lubavitch, I was overjoyed to be able to hear a chassidic discourse. I also heard it repeated three times by the Rebbe's sons and his son-in-law. On Sunday I was in *yechidus* with the Rebbe for over an hour.

The Rebbe expressed his great distress over the trouble being caused by the noblemen who owned the estates and the forests. They harbored resentment toward the Jews, who had leased the [logging rights in] the forests, and who paid high wages to the gentile laborers to cut and transport the lumber. Consequently, the laborers refused to work for the noblemen at lower rates.

"This resentment," [said the Rebbe,] "will raise the level of anti-Semitic feelings and the pogrom spirit that have prevailed during this past year. The Jewish merchants should take this into account — especially those who have taken advantage of the current economic climate to acquire estates and forests from the nobility at very cheap prices."

At the end of the *yechidus*, the Rebbe inquired about my financial situation, and I gave him a very brief summary of how things stand.

"Shmuel, don't give up," replied the Rebbe. "Buy ready-made rafts, also, buy [logs] at the riverbank, and tie them together yourself [to make rafts]. May G-d (blessed be He) send your way good merchandise and honest businessmen — both locally and in Riga — and some side-income in addition."

When I arrived in Rudnia,[7] I bought a ticket to go all the way home. But when I got on the train, I met Reb Aharon Brudna, who was returning from Smolensk, where he had been involved in the dispute between the wealthy Mrs. Dina

---

7. [The train station closest to Lubavitch.]

Wittenberg of Denenburg and the wealthy Mr. Schwartz of Smolensk. They had agreed to a *zabla*, and had already chosen their judges for the *zabla*. Reb Aharon was on his way to see me in Vitebsk, for I was to be the third judge, having been designated by the two chosen judges. We got off the train, and remained in Rudnia to wait for the next train going [in the opposite direction] toward Smolensk.

We labored four days and four nights before we finally succeeded in arranging a compromise and straightening out the particulars of the dispute. I received a generous payment, in the amount of six hundred rubles. I was paid the three hundred from Mr. Schwartz then and there in Smolensk; Reb Aharon Brudna is supposed to send me the three hundred from Mrs. Wittenberg any day.

So you see, my dear Leible, the Rebbe's blessing is already being fulfilled. He blessed me to earn side-income in addition to my business, and (thank G-d) I did earn the income. Leible, one has to be a chassid — then, things are good even in material affairs. I myself (thank G-d) now have some money to pay the grocers, and I will still be left with a few hundred for business expenses.

"But what about the deposit you will have to give to the raft owners?" asked Reb Leib. "And you will also have to pay the oarsmen and the pilots of the rafts. And if you plan to buy [logs] at the riverbank and tie them together by yourself, you will need a fortune — at least several thousand."

"Well, didn't the Rebbe tell me that G-d would send good merchandise my way?" replied Reb Shmuel. "And the holy Rebbe surely knows that you can't buy anything empty-handed! So, it's only reasonable to assume that the blessing includes G-d's sending my way the amount I need to purchase this good merchandise.

"To us chassidim, belief in the sages flows naturally in our veins. We do not need miracles and wonders to prove anything to us. We see the sun in the sky, but none of us has ever investigated or studied it. We have no idea what it is or what this strange object is made of. It has been placed in the sky; but how does it behave, and what sort of thing is it? Yet all of us together know that the sun gives light and benefits all living things; even sick people obtain some relief from their sickness when the sun shines with its maximum power. For chassidim, the Rebbe is their sun, their salvation, and their hope.

"What can I tell you, Leible? We have known each other for thirty years, since we were both young men. You know very well that I was never conceited when things looked up, nor did I ever give up hope when things looked bleak. I always kept in mind that ups and downs are merely parts of a wheel that turns constantly, regardless of whether we are presently on top or on the bottom.

"But this time, I won't hide from you the fact that I am discouraged, and I have almost given up hope entirely. If not for the Rebbe's instructions — transmitted to me by Yisrael Nachman *HaKohen*,[8] the *melamed* in the household of Zalman Yeruchem of Velizh — I would have given up business altogether, and become a rabbi, even in a small village."

"Three days before Pesach I received the first news about my business, and by *Erev* Pesach I already knew that I had fallen into a trap set for me by unscrupulous merchants; I had lost everything I owned, and all that I had borrowed and invested in that unfortunate business.

---

8. [Reb Yisrael Nachman *HaKohen* Mariashin was a great-grandson of Reb Yisrael Nachman Mariasha's; cf. Chapter 8 in *The Making of Chassidim*, Sichos In English, Brooklyn, 1996.]

"It took a great deal of fortitude for me to control my emotions during the first two days of Pesach. During *Chol HaMoed* I nearly went insane, but I resolved that I would put the whole matter out of my mind until after Pesach was over; with G-d's help, I managed to carry out this resolution.

"At the conclusion of the last day of Pesach, I was sick in bed with a high fever for two days. On the third day I felt a little better, and toward evening Yisrael Nachman *HaKohen* of Dubravna came to visit me. He told me that he had come from Lubavitch the previous day, and that the Rebbe had given him a message to deliver to me. I had still been sick when he first arrived; since he was in a hurry to depart for Velizh, he had waited for the first opportunity to deliver the message that the Rebbe had sent. This is what he said:

> During *Chol HaMoed* Pesach, Reb Leivik the butler told me that the Rebbe had said to him, "Although Yisrael Nachman *HaKohen* often departs from Lubavitch without entering for *yechidus*, this time let him not do so"; for the Rebbe wished to send an extremely urgent message with me. When I entered the Rebbe's chamber, I found him sitting in his chair with two *seforim* opened in front of him. As I approached, he covered the open *seforim* with his silk handkerchief, and said to me:
>
> "When you arrive in Vitebsk, go to see Reb Shmuel Brin and inform him that I know everything. I disagree with his decision. On the contrary, I hereby order him to abandon his plans. The Alter Rebbe says that the mind rules over the heart by natural instinct. This applies to the behavior of all people who are worthy of being called human beings. But it especially applies to chassidic behavior. If the heart

obeys the head, then the heart can deal with whatever the head understands.

"Repeat these words to Reb Shmuel Brin in person, and let no one else know about it. If you have to wait a day, do so, but you must transmit the message exactly as I have dictated it. Remember, you've been warned!"

"I understood exactly what the message meant. As soon as I was out of bed, I went to *shul* to *daven*. When I returned, I met Reb Dov Ber Feigelson, from whom I borrowed thirty rubles for my trip. And now, when I receive my three hundred from Denenburg, I will depart on my business trip."

Reb Leib Posen had been sitting there the whole time, listening to Reb Shmuel Brin's story. He could not think of a way to broach the subject of lending him the purse of money, when suddenly his mouth uttered the idea of its own accord:

"Don't worry about capital for your business venture; I've brought you the necessary amount." Before the words were out, he had produced several packets of fifty- and hundred-ruble notes.

Reb Shmuel's eyes wandered from Reb Leib to the packets of notes lying on the table, and back again, but he said nothing. He could not figure out what was the matter with Reb Leib. He was aware that Reb Leib was a philanthropic individual, and that one could always borrow fifty or even a hundred rubles from him. But a sum such as this could hardly be called a casual loan!

"I've brought you a loan of three thousand rubles," said Reb Leib. "I extend the loan until after you've sold the rafts in Riga. Then, you will repay the exact amount; I don't expect any share of the profits."

"What are you talking about, Leible? I can't accept such a loan from you, and you have no right to offer it. Any investment, even the most sound, has the potential for loss as well as profit. G-d forbid that you risk such a sum in someone else's business, and as a free loan yet! In any case, I refuse to take it from you. Who gave you the idea to make me such a proposition?"

Reb Leib Posen then recounted to Reb Shmuel Brin the whole story from beginning to end, while Reb Shmuel paid close attention.

When Reb Leib finished speaking, Reb Shmuel said to him, "You obeyed all the instructions that the Rebbe gave you. 'Good intentions are counted by G-d as if they were deeds,'[9] and in fact He counts it as though the deed was done to perfection. But for my part, I refuse to take the money from you."

That very night Reb Leib Posen traveled to Lubavitch to complain to the Rebbe about Reb Shmuel's refusal to accept the sum as the Rebbe had instructed. He went in to the Rebbe and deposited the packet of notes on the table.

Early Monday morning, the Rebbe's second butler — Reb Pinchas Leib Magidson — came to Reb Shmuel Brin bringing a sealed package that the Rebbe had sent, along with the following note in the Rebbe's handwriting:

"I hereby send to you three thousand rubles to use in your business venture; this loan is extended until after you have sold the rafts in Riga. May you have much success!"

Reb Leib Posen took with him a purse full of money to repay the debts he owed to the merchants in Moscow for the goods he had lost in the fire, and an additional sum to purchase fresh goods. When Reb Leib arrived in Moscow, he began to tell the local merchants about his losses.

---

8. [*Kiddushin* 40a.]

Before he could even finish speaking, one of the leading merchants declared that undoubtedly, they would all be willing to assume a portion of his losses. They would examine their books and let him know what percentage they could afford to discount from his debt. Meanwhile, they would give him as much merchandise as he needed, on credit. A few days later, the merchants informed him that they would cancel fifty percent of the debt, and give him up to two years to pay off the remainder.

That summer, Reb Leib won fifteen thousand rubles in the national lottery. Following the Rebbe's advice, he invested it in linen, acquiring a large quantity of goods at a bargain price. The market price soon rose three-fold. He was equally successful at whatever he put his hand to.

Meanwhile, Reb Shmuel Brin purchased ready-loaded rafts, and also some [logs] tied up on the riverbank. Some [logs] he resold immediately, and some he floated down to Riga as rafts. He earned huge profits and repaid all his debts. Following the Rebbe's advice, he bought a mansion with a large surrounding estate.

Today, Reb Michael Aharon Pisarevsky is quite old. His sons, his daughters, and all his descendants are wealthy business owners.

The chassid Reb Nachman Lipa Zeltzer passed away, leaving behind his sterling reputation and an estate that included mansions, forests, and large business enterprises.

Reb Leib Posen is exceedingly wealthy; his sons are also prosperous, and he is considered one of the aristocracy.

Last but not least — Reb Shmuel Brin left his many businesses to his sons and sons-in-law; he receives an ample income from the mansion that he kept for himself. His home is always open to chassidim, to men of good deeds, and to

Torah scholars. He is held in high esteem even by the *misnagdim*, not to mention by the chassidim.

Reb Meir Mordechai Czernin[1]

BY
THE EDITORS OF *HaTamim*

The history and biography of the chassid Reb Meir Mordechai Czernin really deserve a separate article of their own. Among the stories that he told over a period of many years, some deal with his own history at various stages of his life.

At the age of sixteen, he returned to his home in Borisov from the *yeshivah* in Minsk. The *melamed* Reb Shmuel Dov Ber — known as "Rashdam" — sent for him and delivered to him a note that his father had written several days before his death. This is the text of the note:

> I am about to depart on the journey we all must make. I remind you — Shmuel Dov — of your faithful promise. When my son Meir Mordechai grows up, please repay your debt to me. Teach him *Chassidus* and show him how to follow the chassidic way of life, as I taught it to you and showed it to you. You — my son Meir Mordechai — when you begin studying *Chassidus*, come to visit my grave and tell me about it.

The chassid Reb Meir Mordechai cherished and treasured this note, even in his old age. Referring to this note, the saintly Rebbe Maharash once said: "In these few lines we see

---

1. From *HaTamim*, Issue No. 7, pp. 102-108; 12-13 *Tammuz* 5697. Appeared as a footnote to the story of "Typical Chassidic Businessmen".

a reflection of the radiant personality of a chassidic teacher and mentor."

Reb Meir Mordechai lived through several eras of history. When he passed away, he was remembered with honor in the city of Vitebsk, where he was laid to rest.

Reb Yitzchak
the Tailor's Father[1]

BY
RASHBATZ[2]

From the day that Reb Yitzchak the Tailor became a chassid, he declined to discuss his background. When people asked him about it, he would reply briefly that he was descended from a distinguished family; his paternal grandfather — Reb Meir — had been a prominent *gaon* in his day, whose mouth never ceased speaking words of Torah. His wife had earned the family income.

All of Reb Meir's sons — except Reb Yitzchak's father — had been prominent rabbis of various communities. Only his father had chosen — at the age of eighteen — to marry the daughter of a G-d-fearing villager. He was supported by his father-in-law in the small village for fifteen years, taking advantage of this time to study Torah constantly. Afterwards, he learned to sew, which was how he earned his living.

In his old age, when his hands and legs grew weak and he could no longer work at his trade, he supported himself from a large garden that the nobleman who owned the city

---

1. From *HaTamim*, Issue No. 8, pp. 92-95; 19 *Kislev* 5698, and from material prepared for Issue No. 9 (which never appeared). We have already met Reb Yitzchak the Tailor in the biography of Rashbatz.
2. [The subtitle reads, "From stories told by Rashbatz (whose soul is in *Gan Eden*)." Since Rashbatz passed away in 1905, it is unlikely that the editors of *HaTamim* heard this story directly from him. Probably, it is compiled from notes provided by the Previous Rebbe who, being intimate with Rashbatz, heard the story from him and recorded it in his diary.]

had given him as a gift. Most of the day, however, he spent sitting in the *beis hamedrash* and studying Torah.

Reb Yitzchak related:

> After [my father] married me off, he gave me his house to live in. For himself, he built a three room house: two rooms for his own dwelling, and a third room dedicated as a *beis hamedrash*. Ten elderly Torah scholars sat there studying together, while he provided their material needs.
>
> My father was opposed to the new path [of *avodah*] that had begun to spread throughout that region called *Chassidus*. But to his credit, he took no part in the controversy and feud that broke out at the time.
>
> Once, the *gaon* Reb Shlomo Raphael's came to visit my father. He was one of the foremost opponents of the new path, and corresponded regularly with the *geonim* of the Lithuanian communities. He told my father that this new path was spreading with uncommon speed, and there were already numerous followers in the cities of Vilna, Minsk, Shklov, Slutzk, and others. Some followed this path openly, while others did so in secret.
>
> He also related that in Slutzk, there had lived a renowned *gaon* named Reb Baruch,[3] whom G-d had blessed with great wealth. He had supported numerous Torah scholars, and given charity generously. He had passed away with his reputation intact, but after his passing, it became known that he had been a fol-

---

3. [See the Previous Rebbe's *Memoirs*, Vols. 1 & 2.]

lower of the new path, and had led several innocent Torah scholars astray.

Reb Shlomo Raphael's demanded that my father sign the ban of excommunication which had been issued against the followers of the new path. Father conceded that the leaders of the Jewish people certainly had an obligation to investigate the matter thoroughly, and to pronounce judgment according to the laws of the Torah.

But as for himself, he had gone into exile forty years earlier, and had met a profound Torah scholar who had been a hidden *tzaddik*. They had traveled together for three months, and he had witnessed many wondrous deeds. Before they separated, the man told him three things; one of them was: "Never get involved in any sort of controversy."

This was all that Reb Yitzchak the tailor would say to people, when they inquired about his history.[4]

The chassid Reb Yisrael, Reb Yitzchak's eldest son, could relate at length the story of Reb Yitzchak's father. He heard it all from his second cousin, who had known him well.

Reb Yisrael's paternal grandfather Reb Avraham Shmuel was the third son of the *gaon* and *tzaddik* Reb Meir, who was the patriarch of our family. He possessed outstanding intellectual abilities, on a par with his two older brothers, and he studied Torah diligently day and night. The two older brothers, who had great aptitude and were giants of Torah, married into important families, the daughters of prominent *geonim* of the time.

---

4. However, to Rashbatz he told the story in detail, as we shall see below.

When the period of time that their fathers-in-law had agreed to support them elapsed, they were honored with positions as rabbis of various congregations.

By the time Reb Yisrael's paternal grandfather Reb Avraham Shmuel reached marriageable age, he had earned a reputation as a young genius. People began to suggest to him matches with the daughters of contemporary *geonim*. But he informed his father Reb Meir that he wished to marry the daughter of a villager who would obligate himself to support him for many years. Thus, he would be able to live in seclusion in a small village, and dedicate himself to Torah study with no distractions.

His relatives considered such a marriage beneath the dignity of their distinguished family, and a great quarrel ensued between them over this. But his father, the *tzaddik* Reb Meir, took his son's side in the matter, declaring that since his son's intentions were for the sake of Heaven, his actions were also approved.

One of the estates about forty miles from his town was leased by a tenant named Reb Yosef. He was a sincere, honest, and G-d-fearing person, but of the most undistinguished sort. He could read the prayers and chapters of *Tehillim* only with difficulty, and had no idea at all of what the words meant. G-d had blessed him with sons and daughters, and he had employed a capable *melamed* to teach them. He gave charity generously, and became famous throughout the vicinity for his philanthropy and hospitality. Nevertheless, everyone knew him as a born commoner.

People called him "Yossel *Baruch Hu u'Voruch Sh'mo*,"[5] because of his constant habit of dipping his hands in water, or wiping them on his clothes, and then reciting *Baruch Hu*

---

5. ["Blessed be He, and blessed be His Name," the customary response whenever G-d's Name is mentioned.]

u'Voruch Sh'mo. Whatever he heard, he responded to it with *Amen!* When asked why he had said *Amen,* he would reply that he had heard from a visiting traveler that the Creator (blessed be He) is everywhere, and is always present. Saying *Amen* implies recognition that G-d is our Faithful King.[6]

Reb Yossel heard that the renowned genius — the youngest son of the *gaon* and *tzaddik* Reb Meir — wished to marry the daughter of a simple villager who would support him in his home. He quickly sent his children's *melamed* to inform Reb Meir that he was ready to undertake the obligation of building a house for his exceptional son, and to provide his sustenance for a period of fifteen years. Reb Meir consulted his son about this prospect, and he agreed to it.

A few days later, Reb Yossel and his family came to Szventzian, and the engagement contract was drawn up amidst great joy. When the designated time arrived, a magnificent wedding was held. Reb Avraham Shmuel left his father's home and became a villager, living in the house that his father-in-law built for him — as they had agreed.

Reb Avraham Shmuel studied Torah with much diligence, and greatly enjoyed the total tranquility that living in a small village afforded. On the other hand, he was distressed by his inability to *daven* with a *minyan.* The Jews who lived in the surrounding villages and estates would assemble in his father-in-law's home for public prayer only on *Shabbos.*

The Jews of the neighboring villages were constantly occupied with their labors: some worked the soil, some raised cattle, some ran mills, some were fishermen, and the like. Their entire day was spent in the company of gentiles.

---

6. [The literal meaning of *Amen* is an expression of belief in what has just been said. In the present instance, it may be interpreted as an acronym for *E-l Melech Ne'eman* ("G-d is our Faithful King").]

Nevertheless, they were all G-d-fearing Jews, and most of them had once been knowledgeable in the Torah, having studied in *cheder* or in a *yeshivah* during their youth. It was only the pressures of making a living that had forced them to abandon their studies, but [due these pressures,] they had subsequently forgotten everything.

When Reb Avraham Shmuel moved into the village, he encouraged these Jews to set aside *Shabbos* as a day of communal study. Within a few weeks, the spirit of Torah was apparent throughout the vicinity.

Among the inhabitants of the village and nearby settlement there were three very diligent *bochurim* with outstanding abilities, who had gone to the city to study. When Reb Avraham Shmuel moved to the village, and experienced his great longing to pray with a *minyan*, he proposed to the *bochurim* that they return to the village and *daven* with his *minyan*. In return, he would teach them Torah.

The *bochurim* returned home and became regular members of the *minyan*, which was convened three times a day. Reb Avraham Shmuel kept his promise, studying with them in great depth for several hours daily. After two years passed, the village began to grow. New families settled there, and they built a *shul* where two or three *minyonim* met three times a day to *daven*.

Reb Avraham Shmuel's father-in-law set up a turpentine distillery in the forest, about a mile from the village. There, he built a small house for his daughter and son-in-law, who preferred living away from the noise of the village. Reb Avraham Shmuel would walk to the *shul* three times a day to *daven*.

For fifteen years, Reb Avraham Shmuel sat studying Torah in holiness and purity. He avoided all unnecessary speech, except for extremely brief remarks in cases of great urgency.

During these years, numerous Torah students, scholars, and *geonim* passed through the village. All were astounded by Reb Avraham Shmuel's great stature, the breadth and depth of his knowledge, his righteousness, and his sincerity. His name became well known, and several congregations invited him to serve them as rabbi. But he would not hear of it.

Before the fifteen-year period during which his father-in-law had agreed to support him expired, Reb Avraham Shmuel informed him that he wished to learn a trade by which he might earn his living. For this purpose he had chosen the trade of stitching sacks.

Hearing this, the father-in-law became very upset, and begged him to allow him to continue supporting him. G-d had blessed him with great wealth, and he would be delighted to continue supporting him in his home. But Reb Avraham Shmuel absolutely refused to accept this proposal, insisting that he wished to support himself by the labor of his own hands.

He taught himself to sew, and he and his wife sewed grain and flour sacks, earning an ample income from this trade. While he sewed, Reb Avraham Shmuel reviewed his study of *Gemara-Rashi-Tosafos* by heart. He did this as fluently as if he were reading it from the text.

When a year passed since he had begun to earn money, he made an exact accounting of his profit, after expenses were deducted. He then set aside one tenth of this amount [for charity] with great joy.

They continued living there for three years; in the fourth year they decided to move to Szventzian, the city of Reb Avraham Shmuel's birth. They purchased a small cottage with much surrounding land, where they planted vegetables; his wife had learned to do this as a little girl.

They quickly discovered that sack-stitching was not in great demand in Szventzian, and so Reb Avraham Shmuel learned to be a tailor.

During the twenty years that Reb Avraham Shmuel was away from his hometown, his relatives and friends forgot all about him. The older generation had passed away, and the younger ones had simply forgotten. Some of them had never even known that they had a relative or family acquaintance named Avraham Shmuel, who was the youngest son of the pride of their family, Reb Meir.

Reb Avraham Shmuel, of course, continued to pretend that he was a very simple person, as he worked his trade. Nevertheless, as time passed, people became aware that — beyond his great righteousness and outstanding sincerity — he was an eminent Torah scholar, while his wife excelled in philanthropy and hospitality.

In Szventzian there lived a man named Reb Moshe Gedaliah, who was versed in the Torah, and G-d-fearing. He made his living by purchasing the produce of the fields from the noblemen who owned the estates surrounding Szventzian. Being very poor, he was compelled to sell what he bought immediately, thus operating at a very low profit margin. Quite often, he earned no more than a broker's fee.

Reb Moshe Gedaliah had many sons and daughters to support, and his income was not sufficient to cover his many expenses and the tuition for his sons. He certainly could not afford to have new clothing sewn for him. Eventually, his clothes became completely worn out. The noblemen warned him that if he didn't get himself a new suit, they would not allow him on their property. He therefore tried to think of some plan to obtain new clothes. Hearing that a new, G-d-fearing, tailor had moved to Szventzian about three years earlier, he went to seek his advice.

When Reb Avraham Shmuel learned of Reb Moshe Gedaliah's situation, he offered to sew a new suit for him; he could pay for it a little at a time, as much as he could afford. However, it would be several months before he could complete his work on jobs he had previously accepted. He therefore offered to lend him a suit of his own until then, and to alter it to fit him.

Reb Moshe Gedaliah declined to wear a suit that was not his own. Instead, he proposed to Reb Avraham Shmuel that — since the suit was for business wear — he would accept Reb Avraham Shmuel as a partner [to share in the profits]. Reb Avraham Shmuel declined this offer. But as Reb Moshe Gedaliah refused to accept the suit as a loan, he agreed to sell it to him.

The terms of the sale were that it could be paid out a little at a time, and that he would alter it to fit. Nevertheless, Reb Moshe Gedaliah insisted on paying at least a small amount in cash, and so he pawned the pillow under his head and gave Reb Avraham Shmuel a quarter of a silver ruble as a down payment. He then departed, and Reb Avraham Shmuel blessed him that G-d should send him success in his business.

Reb Moshe Gedaliah resumed his occupation, making the rounds of the noblemen's estates to buy the produce of their land. While traveling, he would fold his new suit and pack it in his knapsack. When he arrived at a nobleman's court, he would remove his torn suit and put on the new suit before entering to see the nobleman.

On the first day that he visited one of the noblemen, he made such a good impression that the nobleman immediately sold him the produce at the first price Reb Moshe

Gedaliah offered. He also agreed to wait a full month for payment, so that he would have time to find a good customer, and thus earn a larger profit.

On the second day, when he approached another nobleman, he had similar success. Here too, he was offered goods at a low price and advantageous terms. Reb Moshe Gedaliah wondered at this, and concluded that the blessing of the G-d-fearing tailor must have been responsible for his success. When he got home, he found good customers, and earned a huge profit.

Little by little, Reb Moshe Gedaliah's income grew. Once, one of the noblemen even sent him to Vilna as his business agent, and he earned an immense sum all at once. After he grew wealthy, he obtained — for his two oldest daughters — sons-in-law who were Torah scholars. Since he now traveled regularly to Vilna, he bought himself a brand new suit of clothes there.[7]

After a few months passed (Reb Moshe Gedaliah was now considered one of the wealthy citizens of Szventzian) he felt that his good fortune had left him, and this distressed him greatly. He told his wife that — although they were still well off — he was not having the same success in business as before. He also described what his financial situation had been when he originally bought the suit from the tailor Reb Avraham Shmuel, and the blessing he had received from him.

"How foolish of you!" exclaimed his wife. "Why did you exchange the G-d-fearing tailor's suit for one that you

---

7. [The article printed in the last issue of *HaTamim* ends here with the promise "To be continued." Material for the remainder of the story was prepared for the next issue, which was never printed. It is translated here from that material, which was discovered in the Previous Rebbe's library (see Translator's Introduction).]

bought in Vilna? It must be that garment which brought you favor and success."

She then went to look for the suit, cleaned and pressed it, and gave it to her husband to put on when needed. Reb Moshe Gedaliah now discovered that it was true: the tailor's suit was responsible for his success in business.

Reb Moshe Gedaliah's wife was a chatterbox; she told the story to her married sisters, and her sisters told their husbands. One of them scoffed at the idea, but the other one took it seriously. He sought out the tailor Reb Avraham Shmuel, and went to see him and ask him to sew a new suit for him. Reb Avraham Shmuel replied that he was leaving town, and would not have time to sew any new clothes.

Having no other choice, the man begged him at least to give him one of his own suits, and alter it to fit him. Reb Avraham Shmuel agreed to this, and showed him one of his old garments, which found favor in the man's eyes. Three days later, the man returned and took the garment that Reb Avraham Shmuel had altered, and he put it on. Reb Avraham Shmuel blessed him that G-d grant him success in all his undertakings.

Reb Avraham Shmuel was greatly distressed by the fact that he had been married for many years but was still childless. In fact, his wife had conceived several times, but she had always miscarried.

Reb Avraham Shmuel blamed this on his own sins, and decided to go into exile for one year as penance. Perhaps G-d would then take pity upon him and grant him living children. He informed his wife of this plan, and she consented to it. That was why he had told Reb Moshe Gedaliah's brother-in-law that he was leaving town.

From the first day that Reb Moshe Gedaliah's brother-in-law (his name was Reb Baruch Shlomo) put on Reb

Avraham Shmuel's garment, he began to have success in business, and he realized that the story he had been told was true.

Little by little, the story became public knowledge, and multitudes flocked to the tailor's doorstep. To their great disappointment, they discovered that he was gone. This now became the talk of the town: Reb Avraham Shmuel the tailor, the son of the *gaon* and *tzaddik* Reb Meir, was himself a hidden *tzaddik*. People awaited his return with much anticipation.

Meanwhile, Reb Avraham Shmuel went into exile. He fasted constantly, and afflicted his body with severe forms of self-torment. Since he insisted on supporting himself solely by the labor of his own hands, he would mend clothes in the towns through which he passed.

Once, Reb Avraham Shmuel met a poor man named Reb Mordechai,[8] who was an outstanding Torah scholar. Reb Avraham Shmuel was delighted to listen to his Torah discussions and his profound novel insights, and he developed a great love for him. But when Reb Avraham Shmuel observed Reb Mordechai's conduct, he discovered that his ways were quite eccentric.

Reb Mordechai refused to accept donations, and made do with whatever he had. Therefore, he concluded that Reb Mordechai was not a wandering beggar, but must be in exile like himself. Thus, he found it strange that he never saw Reb Mordechai afflict himself with self-torments or fasting.

Before each prayer, Reb Mordechai would disappear for quite some time. Although Reb Avraham Shmuel articulated each word audibly as he prayed, Reb Mordechai's prayer

---

8. [This Reb Mordechai may very well have been the great scholar, *tzaddik*, and *kabbalist* Reb Mordechai Bayever. See *The Making of Chassidim*, Sichos In English, Brooklyn, 1996.]

took much longer than own. He also spent several hours a day studying by heart: his lips moved, but no sound escaped them.

One day, as they were traveling alone through the countryside, Reb Mordechai told Reb Avraham Shmuel that he wished to prepare himself to *daven Minchah*. He put down his knapsack and began to walk through the field. When Reb Avraham Shmuel asked where he was going, he replied that he was going to look for a river or stream in which to immerse himself, for it was his habit always to immerse himself before *davening*, summer or winter. Reb Avraham Shmuel said that he would go along with him, for he wished to take a swim to relieve the heat of the day.

After they had gone some distance, Reb Mordechai saw a brook bubbling a short distance away; he stopped walking and removed his clothes. Reb Avraham Shmuel saw nothing, and looked at Reb Mordechai as if he had lost his mind. Reb Mordechai instructed him to walk back ten paces, and to wait for him there.

When Reb Mordechai returned a short while later, his face and hair were dripping wet, as though he had just emerged from a bath. Reb Avraham Shmuel found this quite amazing, but Reb Mordechai said, "Why are you so astonished? Didn't the Sages tell us[9] that 'If one wishes to purify himself, Heaven comes to his aid'? Now it is known in Heaven that for many years I purify myself before each prayer. Therefore, G-d (blessed be He), caused the water to bubble up from the depths of the earth, just so I would be able to immerse myself."

From then on, Reb Avraham Shmuel began to emulate Reb Mordechai's ways. He realized that this must be one of the hidden *tzaddikim*, and that beyond his great knowledge

---

9. [*Yoma* 38b.]

of the revealed Torah, he also possessed deep knowledge of *Kabbalah*. Reb Mordechai offered to teach Reb Avraham Shmuel *Kabbalah*, and they studied together several times. But later, Reb Avraham Shmuel declined to continue, saying that he would soon be returning home. If he then continued studying *Kabbalah* on his own, he would surely get it wrong; therefore, he thought it best not to begin studying this subject at all.

Before they went their separate ways, Reb Mordechai told Reb Avraham Shmuel three things:

a) do not refuse a request made by the whole community;
b) when a son is born to you, name him Yitzchak;
c) never get involved in any sort of controversy.

Reb Avraham Shmuel returned home in time for Shavuos, without anyone being aware of it. His wife reported to him the stories that had been spread in the city about him: his garments served as charms to bring the wearer favor and success, and many of the townsfolk eagerly awaited his return. This disturbed him greatly, and he therefore decided to abandon the tailor's trade and to take up the trade of repairing old utensils instead. He had learned this craft during his journeys in exile, and could now make a good living at it.

After a few weeks, it became known that the tailor had returned home. The first person to come to him was Reb Moshe Gedaliah's second brother-in-law, Reb David, who had scoffed upon first hearing the stories about the tailor. He now envied his brother-in-law Reb Baruch Shlomo, who had become very successful after purchasing the suit from Reb Avraham Shmuel. When he came, he found him repairing old utensils, and asked, "Where is the tailor?"

"There is no tailor living here," replied Reb Avraham Shmuel. Reb David returned home and investigated the matter. He then discovered that this person was none other than the tailor, but that he had changed his occupation, and now repaired utensils.

Meanwhile, the governor of the city heard the rumor of the tailor in his city, who was a great *tzaddik*, and who sewed garments that gave favor and success. He commanded his superintendent to harness the horses, ride to the city, and summon the tailor to his court.

When the tailor's wife saw the opulent carriage pull up to their door, and a uniformed official descend from it, she grew very frightened and told her husband about it. When Reb Avraham Shmuel heard the message of the governor's agent, he replied that he was unaccustomed to riding in such a lavish conveyance. If it was all the same to the governor, he would prefer to come to him on foot. To this, the official agreed. A few days later, Reb Avraham Shmuel took his knapsack and went to the governor's court.

The governor expressed his desire to have Reb Avraham Shmuel sew him a new suit. To this, Reb Avraham Shmuel replied that he had indeed once sewn clothes, but he had since abandoned that occupation and now repaired old utensils. Reb Avraham Shmuel made a favorable impression on the governor, who had a kindly disposition and was friendly toward the Jews. Seeing that Reb Avraham Shmuel was reluctant to resume his tailoring, he didn't press the issue, and sent him on his way.

During the following month of Av a fire broke out in the city and two thirds of the city burned down, including the four *shuls* and the stores in the marketplace. Hundreds of people were left homeless and starving.

The governor sent ten wagons loaded with potatoes and other vegetables, and two wagons loaded with flour, to be distributed to the victims of the fire. He also invited the president of the Jewish community to send about a hundred people to live on his estate until new homes could be built for them.

The president and several town dignitaries went to thank the governor for his kindness and generosity to the fire victims. The governor then gave them permission to cut lumber from his large forest to rebuild the burned homes.

"In about three months' time," said the governor, "there will be a convention of the nobility in Vilna. I would be pleased if the tailor who lives in your community — who sews garments that have a charm of favor and success — were to sew for me a new suit. If he did so, then besides paying his fee, I would also donate — free of charge — lumber to rebuild the four synagogues that burned down."

The president convened a mass meeting, and told the assembly all about the governor's great kindness and generosity in allowing all the fire victims to take lumber from his forest to rebuild their homes. All those present blessed the governor for this. The president then told them of the governor's request to the tailor.

They decided to summon the tailor and beg him to do this thing, for it was for the good of the whole community. When Reb Avraham Shmuel heard the community's request, he refused at first. But he quickly remembered Reb Mordechai's instruction: "Do not refuse a request made by the whole community," and so he agreed.

The president and Reb Avraham Shmuel went to see the governor, who received them with great honor. He gave Reb Avraham Shmuel cloth, and showed him the design of his old clothes, requesting him to make the new suit in the same style. Two weeks later, Reb Avraham Shmuel brought the new suit to the governor, and blessed him to have success in all his affairs.

The governor's servants then brought the lumber and building supplies, and assisted the Jewish builders in rebuilding the *shuls*. They worked in great haste, so that the first *shul* could be ready for the High Holy Days. The governor also added a parcel of land to Reb Avraham Shmuel's lot, and ordered his servants to build a house for him.

During the month of Cheshvan, Reb Avraham Shmuel's wife discovered that she was pregnant. She wept bitterly as she recalled her many miscarriages, and so she went to visit the grave of her father-in-law, the *tzaddik* Reb Meir, and poured out her heart there. Her husband Reb Avraham Shmuel also gave her verbal support.

One night, she dreamed that an old man came to her and admonished her: "Why do you weep? You have conceived, and you will give birth to a son. Change your mood, and rejoice."

When she awoke, she could still see the old man's face before her eyes, and she reported it to her husband. Reb Avraham Shmuel then recalled what the *tzaddik* Reb Mordechai had told him, and he related to his wife what had happened to him during his exile with the poor man who was a hidden *tzaddik*. She rejoiced very much at this, for she believed in G-d and in His servants, the holy *tzaddikim*.

At the convention of noblemen and government ministers in Vilna, the governor of the city of Szventzian was elected governor over all of Vilna County. All the Jews of the vicinity rejoiced at this.

The governor of the city and all of Vilna kept his promise in full, donating the building supplies for the remaining three *shuls*, and continuing to act kindly toward the Jews who lived in his city. The very first thing he did, was to enter a law on the books that Reb Avraham Shmuel was exempt from paying taxes, and that the serfs of his estate were to plant and harvest Reb Avraham Shmuel's garden for free.

When construction of the fourth *shul* was completed, Reb Avraham Shmuel's wife gave birth to a son, whom they named Yitzchak.

Appendix A:

Letter from the Rebbe Maharash with Remarks by the Previous Rebbe[1]

A Collection[2] of Sacred Handwritten Letters by My Saintly Grandfather, the Rebbe Maharash:

Bibliographic Remarks[3]

The present letter was handwritten by my saintly grandfather, the Rebbe Maharash. It was written in Marienbad during the month of Menachem Av 5628 [July 1868]. The letter is marked "public-private,"[4] and was addressed to the city of Borisov. It was delivered Wednesday 10 Menachem Av, 5628 [July 29, 1868] to the address of one of the elder chassidim — and leading member of the community — the

---

1. From *HaTamim*, Issue No. 5, pp. 8-10, published in conjunction with the story of Rashdam. The editors of *HaTamim* inserted the following introductory remarks at the beginning of this article:

    We herewith present a letter written by the Rebbe Maharash of holy and blessed memory, together with introductory bibliographic remarks by his grandson the Lubavitcher Rebbe *Shlita*, describing the origins and content of the letter. The beginning and end of the letter are reproduced in facsimile from the original manuscript.

2. The sacred handwritten manuscripts are stored in special collections. There is a separate collection for each Rebbe, where his holy letters are deposited.
3. Each sacred manuscript in the collection has an attached note authenticating its origin and describing its history.
4. "Public" letters are those written to all *Anash* wherever they live. Letters sent to *Anash* of a specific city are marked "public-private.".

chassid and doer of good deeds, Reb Leib Aizik (of blessed memory).

Subject of the letter:

i) The necessity of having a specific person appointed as *mashpia*, to teach *Chassidus* and to arouse people's hearts to the service of G-d (blessed be He).
ii) The obligation and the capability of business people to engage in *avodah*.
iii) Authorization of the chassid Reb Shmuel Dov Ber as *mashpia*.

Thanks to the efforts of the chassid Reb Meir Mordechai Czernin of Borisov (one of Reb Shmuel Dov Ber's pupils), the sons of the chassid Reb Leib Aizik (the chassidim Reb Yehoshua and Reb Michel) were persuaded to bring this letter as a gift to my saintly father the Rebbe [Rashab] when they came to Lubavitch for the *Shabbos Parshas Shelach* 5650 [June 14, 1890]. The aforementioned chassid Reb Meir Mordechai told me the whole story of this affair in detail.

Description and size of the letter:

The letter is written on blue paper, size 29 X 22.5 cm. It contains nineteen lines: the first line contains *BH* and the date and place it was written; the next two lines list the persons to whom it was addressed; the body of the letter contains fifteen lines; the last line is the signature.

APPENDIX A

Text of the letter

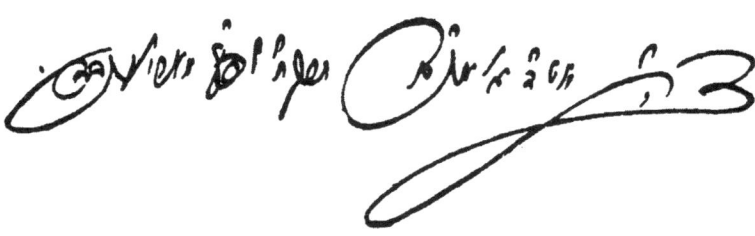

BH Wednesday, 3 Menachem Av 5628 [July 22, 1868], Marienbad:

To my esteemed intimate comrades, the general public,[5] the outstanding veteran chassidim of the Congregation of Borisov. Especially, to my esteemed and beloved comrades, the outstanding veteran chassidim, renowned and noble, Reb Leib Aizik, Reb Avraham Merzin, Reb Zalman Lipshitz, Reb Chayim Asher, and his brother-in-law Reb Dov Ber Landau.[6]

Greetings, and may you all be well;

You esteemed gentlemen are surely aware that we are living in hard times, especially during the present year when inflation is running rampant.[7] Therefore I have decided to write these few lines to beg you all in the strongest terms to keep in mind our outstanding friend, the noted chassid Reb Shmuel Dov Ber, who dwells in your community. My saintly

---

5. As we know, my saintly grandfather the Rebbe Maharash was very careful in his speech, and even more so in his writing. This holds true not only for his chassidic discourses, but also for his letters. The usual style for beginning a letter such as this one would be: *To my esteemed intimate comrades, the outstanding veteran* chassidim *of the Congregation of Borisov.* However, my grandfather added the words *the general public,* for the subject of this letter deals with the necessity of designating a *mashpia*, and of business people engaging in *avodah*; these subjects are of concern to "the general public".
6. According to the aforementioned chassid Reb M. M. C., these five men were the elder chassidim in Borisov, and all of them held great influence in the city.
7. There was a drought during that year, and the produce of all the fields and gardens was ruined for lack of rain.

father [the *Tzemach Tzedek*] spoke to me on numerous occasions about this chassid, describing him with the greatest praise, and mentioning especially the fact that he once dwelt in our courtyard.[8] Later, he often spoke of him more highly than of any of his contemporaries.

Now the fact is that each one of *Anash* needs to have a person specifically designated to teach *Chassidus*, explaining it in public lectures and in private lessons. This person must also arouse the hearts of the chassidim, so that the element of love of G-d that lies hidden within the heart of every Jew becomes activated from potential to actual, and so that each may serve G-d with fear and with love etc., according to his own abilities. This is even more necessary in these hard times, when each person's mind and heart are occupied with his personal problems.

Let the businessman not say, "But I am busy and preoccupied, so how can such ideas penetrate my heart?" It is not so! On the contrary, business people have it within their capacity — and for them it is even easier — to serve the Creator whenever the opportunity presents itself, as explained in detail in several places in *Sefer Shel Beinonim* [*Tanya*], in *Derech HaChayim*, and in *Likkutei Torah*. Study the discourse beginning with the words[9] "As an apple tree among the trees of the forest...," which was recited during the years 5619 and 5621[10] (I remember that the aforementioned Reb Shmuel Dov heard it recited). The main thing is

---

8. During Elul 5616 [August 1856], a great fire broke out in Lubavitch (may such a disaster not befall us). In this fire most of the buildings in town were burned down, including the holy courtyard containing the houses of my saintly great-grandfather the *Tzemach Tzedek*, my saintly grandfather the Rebbe Maharash, and my saintly great-uncles, the *tzaddikim* who were the *Tzemach Tzedek's* sons. Afterwards, the *Tzemach Tzedek* lived in a large courtyard on the outskirts of the city until the houses could be rebuilt.
9. [*Shir HaShirim* 2:3.]
10. [See *Or HaTorah, Shir HaShirim*, Vol. I, p. 189.]

Appendix A

that one should have the desired intentions, as explained in several places, including the discourse beginning with the words, "All people of Israel."[11]

For the above reasons, I now submit the following request: see to it that there is some central location where communal funds — as well as additional funds contributed by private individuals — may be deposited. Make it an inviolable rule that each week this money be collected for our aforementioned intimate comrade, so that he may have an income without cares in his old age,[12] thus enabling him to devote his time to the study of *Chassidus*. This will be to your own benefit as well. Though he is willing to teach you even without this, it is not the same thing at all, as the wise will readily understand. This is even more important in view of the fact that the citizens of your town are presently in need of a rabbinic authority. I am certain that you will all assemble for this purpose, to appropriate a regular salary to be paid [to the rabbi] from some community fund. And so, it is my urgent request that at the same time you also make regular collections for the present purpose [Reb Shmuel Dov's support] — at least the sum of three or four silver rubles a week[13] — so that his monetary worries are relieved. See *Midrash Rabbah, Parshas Behar*, section 34.[14]

---

11. [See *Sefer HaMaamarim 5626*, p. 168, 170.]
12. Apparently, in the year 5628 Reb Shmuel Dov was already considered one of the elder chassidim. [He was actually sixty years old at the time.]
13. The chassid Reb M. C. related that they then appropriated a salary of seven silver rubles a week for the *mashpia*, to be collected from an assessment of private individuals; an additional three silver rubles were obtained from the community treasury.
14. My saintly grandfather, the Rebbe [Maharash] wrote simply "section 34," without indicating a specific passage. In fact, the whole section speaks about charity and about supporting Torah scholars. Nevertheless there are numerous passages, and he ought to have cited a specific passage. But he deliberately declined to do so, allowing each individual to locate the passage that applies to him personally.

I trust that you will give due attention to these earnestly spoken words of mine, and that you will fulfill my request. Please inform me of the results; I will give you an address in Odessa [where the reply may be sent]. In reward for all this, may G-d bless all your undertakings, as Scripture states in *Parshas Reeh*, 16:14, "You shall surely give... in reward for this the L—rd your G-d will bless you in all your deeds and all your undertakings."

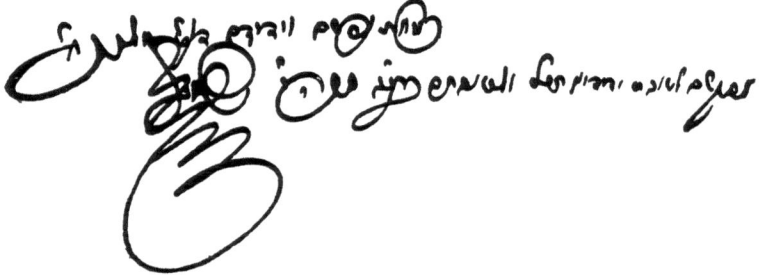

As you yourselves desire, so do I, your intimate comrade who seeks your welfare as the desire of my heart and soul. I beg you [to obey my instructions] for the benefit of our aforementioned comrade, and also for your own spiritual and material benefit, forever each day.

[signed]: Shmuel.

Appendix B:

Letter from the *Tzemach Tzedek* with Remarks by the Previous Rebbe, and Excerpts from His Diary[1]

Excerpt from the Diary of the Lubavitcher Rebbe, *Shlita:*

Monday, 16 *Teves*, 5688 [January 9, 1928], Riga.

Today, I received by post a gift from the estate of the late renowned chassid Reb Avraham Abba Persan of Königsberg: some holy handwritten letters and chassidic discourses.

---

1. From *HaTamim*, Issue No 6, pp. 6-12, published in conjunction with the stories of Reb Chayim Yehoshua, Reb Gavriel *Nossai Chein*, and the Vilenker Brothers. The editors of *HaTamim* inserted the following introductory remarks at the beginning of this article:

    We herewith present a facsimile of a letter written by the saintly Lubavitcher Rebbe the *Tzemach Tzedek*, that we were fortunate enough to receive from the office of the Lubavitcher Rebbe, *Shlita*'s personal library. The original of this letter is deposited in a special collection of holy letters written by the *Tzemach Tzedek*. Attached to it are an excerpt from the Rebbe's diary describing the history of this handwritten manuscript, and a detailed analysis of the authenticity and contents of the letter, entitled "Bibliographic Remarks."

    The following are, in order, the excerpt from the diary, the bibliographic remarks, as they were given to us, and the facsimile.

As soon as I arrived in Riga I began to inquire about the estate of the gracious chassid mentioned above. Today (thank G-d), I have succeeded in obtaining handwritten manuscripts by: my great-grandfather the holy Rebbe the *Tzemach Tzedek;* the holy rabbis and *tzaddikim,* my great-uncles, sons of the *Tzemach Tzedek;* my grandfather, the holy Rebbe Reb Yosef Yitzchak;[2] my grandfather, the holy Rebbe Reb Shmuel,[3] and my saintly father the holy Rebbe [Rashab]. A detailed list is attached.

Bibliographic Remarks

Wednesday, 25 *Teves*, 5688 [January 18, 1828].

A letter written in the holy handwriting of my saintly great-grandfather the *Tzemach Tzedek.* He wrote it to the well-known chassidic magnate, Reb Zev Volf Vilenkes. The chassid Reb Zev Volf once ran many business enterprises in the city of Vitebsk, and owned a very large store. He was also involved in the forestry business. The entire managerial staff of his commercial establishment was made up of chassidim and men of good deeds.

The chassidic magnate Reb Zev Volf was very involved in communal affairs, and his name was familiar to the most important civic leaders. He was very wise, and strong-willed. He was frequently summoned to the government offices by the governor-general [of Vitebsk], who would reprimand him and warn him about the conduct of the Jews who resided in the city, or in the whole district.

I first learned of the existence of this letter from Reb Avraham Abba Persan during the summer of 5661 [1901],

---

2. [Of Avruch, son of the *Tzemach Tzedek.* He was the Previous Rebbe's maternal grandfather, after whom the Previous Rebbe was named.]
3. [The Rebbe Maharash.]

APPENDIX B

when we happened to meet in Warsaw (as described in my diary of 5661). He told me that the Rebbe the *Tzemach Tzedek* wrote the letter in the year 5605 [1845], two years after his first summons to a Rabbinical Convention in Petersburg in 1843 — 5603. The letter was written in great secrecy, because they were very afraid of the government officials. That was the fourth year that a high-ranking police official had been stationed in Lubavitch (which was, after all, only a small hamlet among other rural villages). His orders were to keep an eye on the activities of the Rebbe and those who visited him.

In the year 5602 [1842], the governor-general of Vitebsk was informed — by Yisrael Yosef, the snatcher of Bichev — that my holy great-grandfather the Rebbe had sent the outstanding young scholar Reb Aharon of Bilinycz as his agent to all communities in the counties of Mohilev and Vitebsk. Most of the leaders of these communities were chassidim. He instructed them that they were to expel the snatchers from their midst and excommunicate them, for they had resumed their child snatching after a two-year interruption.

The governor of Vitebsk informed the Minister of Internal Affairs about this, and for that reason the Rebbe was summoned to Petersburg for the first time, during the summer of 5603. Their intention was to indict him for high treason. But in order to disguise their intentions, they resorted to a ruse, summoning three others in addition: the *gaon* Reb Y. of Volozhin, Reb Y. Halperin, and the *Maskil* Betzalel Stern. The proceedings of that Rabbinical convention are well known, and are recorded elsewhere. From that time on, the government kept a closer watch over the Rebbe the *Tzemach Tzedek*.

All this did not affect the Rebbe, who simply ignored it. He continued his practice of sending his emissaries to encourage those who were in military service to observe the Torah and its *mitzvos*, and he sent his agents to ransom the cantonists.[4] He also took part in a plot to eradicate the snatchers. Alas, during the year 5605 a misfortune occurred: the chassid Reb Chayim Yehoshua of Kalisk was caught red-handed, ransoming a few cantonists for a large sum of money in the village of Kastoreve, near Kazan, in central Russia.

The present letter was sent by my great-grandfather, the Rebbe the *Tzemach Tzedek*, to the chassid Reb Zev Volf. It refers to the matter of Reb Chayim Yehoshua, and his rescue. I saw the letter in the possession of the chassid Reb Avraham Abba Persan, when my family and I were living in Königsberg during the summer of 5668 [1908], as mentioned in my diary.

The following is what Reb Avraham Abba related to me in connection with this holy letter:

"When we happened to meet in Warsaw during the summer of 5661, I told you about this letter. It was written by the Rebbe the *Tzemach Tzedek* to my father-in-law's father-in-law (that is how he always referred to his wife's maternal grandfather), the chassid Reb Zev Volf Vilenkes. Now that we have it in our possession, I will explain it word by word, exactly as I heard it and as [the commentary] was transmitted to me."

A COLLECTION OF SACRED HANDWRITTEN LETTERS BY MY SAINTLY GREAT-GRANDFATHER, THE REBBE THE *TZEMACH TZEDEK* (OF HOLY AND BLESSED MEMORY)

Translator's note: As mentioned previously, "The letter was written in great secrecy, because they were very afraid of the

---

4. Jewish children who were handed over by the snatchers for twenty-five years' military service were called "Cantonists".

Appendix B

government officials..." Therefore, the letter does not mention Reb Chayim Yehoshua by name, nor does it refer specifically to his arrest or rescue. On its surface, the letter seems to be an appeal for financial assistance in behalf of "the bearer," Reb Sender Yechiel. Thus, if the letter were to fall into the wrong hands, it contains nothing to implicate the *Tzemach Tzedek* (or anyone else) in a plot to rescue an accused traitor.

Text of the *Tzemach Tzedek's* letter (footnotes to this text represent the Previous Rebbe's commentary, as he heard it from Reb Avraham Abba Persan):

To my beloved staunch and intimate comrade,[5] namely the outstanding rabbinic personality, the veteran man of

---

5. The Rebbe [the *Tzemach Tzedek*] knew thousands of chassidim of his grandfather, the Alter Rebbe, and his father-in-law, the Mitteler Rebbe. Of these, there were only a very few individuals upon whom he conferred the title "my beloved staunch and intimate comrade." Commenting on the verse, "G-d gives strength to His people," the Rabbis of blessed memory say that the term "strength" refers exclusively to Torah [*translator's note*: the Hebrew term for "staunch" in this letter, is the same word used in this verse for "strength"].

I have heard six stories, all based on the same theme: during the first eighteen years that the Mitteler Rebbe and the *Tzemach Tzedek* lived in Lubavitch —

intellect..., the honorable Rabbi Zev Volf (may your brilliance shine forth):

I make a great request of you, and beg you [to act] in behalf of one whom I love as my own soul,[6] as a friend and brother, the bearer of this note[7] (may his brilliance shine forth). Look after him with an open eye,[8] with all your heart[9] and soul. Come to his aid with acts of charity.[10] Do this for my sake...[11] remembering the friendship of our youth.[12] May

---

        beginning in 5574 [1814] — the chassid Reb Zev Volf bought and sold merchandise as the *Tzemach Tzedek's* business partner. The *Tzemach Tzedek* lent him a sum of money, and received a share of the profits. Thus, the *Tzemach Tzedek* was able to devote himself to Torah and *avodah*, and to support his sons, the saintly *tzaddikim*, with affluence. This income was in addition to the allowance he received from his saintly father-in-law, the Mitteler Rebbe.

6. All these titles refer to the chassid Reb Chayim Yehoshua (whose soul is in *Gan Eden*), who risked his life to ransom the cantonists in various localities. He occupied himself with this mission for eight years, securing the release of hundreds of children, until he was caught in a trap by the wicked spy from Vohlynia.

7. The messenger was Reb Sender Yechiel of Dubravna, who was an agent of my saintly great-grandfather the *Tzemach Tzedek*. He was sent to encourage those in military service to remain steadfast in their faith and to observe the precepts of their religion. He would also give financial aid to those who needed it. The Rebbe sent Reb Sender Yechiel to Reb Zev Volf with instructions as to how he should proceed with the rescue of Reb Chayim Yehoshua.

8. The chassid Reb Chayim Yehoshua was imprisoned under very harsh conditions. At first the governor wanted him tried for treason by a military court, and he boasted that he would execute Reb Chayim Yehoshua by hanging. It took a great deal of persuasion to influence him to hold the trial in civil court. Therefore, the Rebbe urged him to "Look after him with an open eye," and remain alert to prevent the governor from carrying out his wicked intent.

9. The chassid Reb Zev Volf was highly intellectual and strong-willed, avoiding emotion at all costs. Therefore, the Rebbe hinted to him that — on occasion — one's emotions must take precedence over the intellect.

10. In reward for Reb Chayim Yehoshua's charitable act of risking his life for *pidyon sh'vuyim*; the same charity must now be shown to him attempting his rescue.

11. At the secret meeting convened by my great-grandfather the *Tzemach Tzedek* in 5594 [1834] to discuss ways of dealing with the problem of the cantonists and the snatchers, Reb Zev Volf was one of those who recommended that the Rebbe not be involved in the affair. He was afraid that it would eventually be

the Father of Mercy[13] invoke His mercy upon us, and may the Source[14] of All Blessings bestow upon you the blessing of the three-stranded thread:[15] children, long life, and sustenance; as you yourself desire, and as I desire, who have loved you from the very beginning, seeking your welfare as the desire of my own heart and soul. I beg this favor of you from the depths of my being.

                              [signed]: Menachem[16]

---

      discovered, and much trouble would come of it. But the Rebbe insisted that he was obligated by law to involve himself personally. He cited several proofs from cases where his grandfather the Alter Rebbe, and his father-in-law the Mitteler Rebbe, had done so. Therefore, he now wrote, "Do this for my sake" — for Reb Chayim Yehoshua was not the only one in prison; in fact, the Rebbe himself was at risk of being imprisoned.

12. When the chassid Reb Zev Volf had his first *yechidus* with the Alter Rebbe, he requested a program whereby he could atone for the sins of his youth. To this, the Alter Rebbe had replied, "Your atonement for the sins of your youth may be achieved by doing a *mitzvah*, based simply on accepting the yoke of the kingdom of Heaven, even when it is contrary to the dictates of your own intellect." The Rebbe was reminding him of this by his reference to "the friendship *of our youth*."

13. The difference between "Father of Mercy" and "Merciful Father" is well known. The former belongs to the *sefirah* of *chochmah*, which is the first stage in the evolutionary progression of creation. The latter belongs to the *sefirah* of *kesser*, which is higher than the progression of creation; i.e., it is derived from the Infinite Luminary (blessed be He), Who is higher than all worlds, and is the "Source of all Blessings." This is explained in a [chassidic] commentary on the expression "May it be Your Will"; [this expression] draws down a newly-conceived will [of G-d] to grant all our requests.

14. It is drawn down from the level of *kesser*, which is higher than the evolutionary progression of creation [see previous note]. Consequently, it is derived from "the Source of All Blessings."

15. This is a synonym for "drawing down," like the "ray and strand" [referred to in *Kabbalah*]. It is called the "three-stranded thread" because the drawing down of the Source of All Blessings — which is the level of *kesser* — is achieved through the three columns upon which the world stands. This is true for the world in general, and also for each individual person: his personal "world" stands upon the three columns of children, long life, and sustenance.

16. My saintly great-grandfather the *Tzemach Tzedek* used five different forms of his signature: i) "Menachem Mendel ben Devorah Leah"; ii) "Menachem

[P.S.]: Please convey my greetings to one whom I love as my own soul, the outstanding rabbinic personality, the wealthy, prominent, and philanthropic Reb Gavriel, (may his brilliance shine forth).

Mendel ben Devorah Leah, grandson of my saintly grandfather, the G-dly *gaon*, of blessed memory"; iii) "Menachem Mendel"; iv) "Menachem Mendel," with loops appended to the signature; v) "Menachem," with loops appended to the signature. My saintly grandfather Reb Shmuel [the Rebbe Maharash] explained the significance of these different forms of his signature, as I have written in detail in my diary. Here, there are five loops, consisting of ten half-circles.

APPENDIX C:

CHASSIDIC DISCOURSE ON THE SUBJECT OF "SHINING"[1]

STORY TOLD BY REB AVRAHAM ABBA PERSAN

I was in Lubavitch visiting the Rebbe the *Tzemach Tzedek* during the festival of Shavuos 5621, which fell on Wednesday and Thursday [May 15 and 16, 1861]. During the festive meal on the second day of *Yom Tov*, which was held in the small *shul*, I was privileged to stand next to the *Tzemach Tzedek's* son, Reb Chayim Schneur Zalman.[2]

The order of seating was as follows: The Rebbe sat at the head of the table. The Rebbe's brother-in-law Reb Menachem Nachum, who was a son of the Mitteler Rebbe,[3] had come for Shavuos, and he sat at the Rebbe's right; continuing down the right side, sat in order: the Rebbe's second son, the *tzaddik* Reb Yehudah Leib;[4] his brother, the *tzaddik* Reb Yisrael Noach;[5] his brother, Reb Shmuel.[6] At the Rebbe's left sat in order: the Rebbe's eldest son, the *tzaddik* Reb Baruch Shalom; his brother, the *tzaddik* Reb Chayim Schneur

---

1. From *HaTamim*, Issue No. 6, pp. 89-97; 2 & 13 Nissan 5697; excerpted from the story of Reb Gavriel *Nossai Chein*.
2. [The Rebbe's third son, who later served as the Rebbe of Liadi.]
3. His home was in the city of Niezhin, in the Ukraine.
4. [Who later served as the Rebbe of Kapust.]
5. [The Rebbe's fourth son; he was the son-in-law of his uncle Reb Menachem Nachum, and later served as the Rebbe of Niezhin. He was the father of the Previous Rebbe's father-in-law.]
6. [The Rebbe's youngest son, who later became the Rebbe Maharash of Lubavitch; he was the Previous Rebbe's paternal grandfather.]

Zalman; his brother, the *tzaddik* Reb Yosef Yitzchak.[7] The Rebbe's sons-in-law were not present on that occasion; therefore, the Rebbe's grandchildren sat further down the table, after his sons; further still, sat elder chassidim and prominent rabbis.

Since I had the good fortune to stand next to the chair of Reb Chayim Schneur Zalman, I was positioned only two chairs distant from the Rebbe's holy seat. Thus, I was able to hear every word that issued from his holy mouth. The things I saw and heard during that Shavuos festival make a story of their own, and this is not the appropriate place to tell it. Here, I will only relate what pertains to our story about Reb Gavriel.

The Rebbe began his remarks by saying: "During the festive meal of the second day of Shavuos 5555 [Monday, May 25, 1795], when I was six years old, my saintly grandfather[8] remarked that during the festive meal of the second day of Shavuos 5528 [Monday, May 23, 1768], his holy Rebbe[9] said: '[It is written], "You shall count for yourselves..." — the term "you shall count" also shares a connection to the concepts of shining and brilliance.[10] "You shall count for yourselves" thus can be interpreted as: See to it that your "self" is shining.'

"My saintly grandfather then leaned upon his elbows and sang the '*Niggun* of the Four Stanzas'[11] with great *deveikus*. Afterwards, he raised his holy head and said, in the traditional melody of a [Talmudic] query: 'And with what

---

7. [The Rebbe's fifth son, who later served as the Rebbe of Avruch; he was the Previous Rebbe's maternal grandfather.]
8. The Alter Rebbe, author of the *Tanya*.
9. The *Maggid* of Mezritch.
10. [A play on words: the Hebrew words for "counting" and "shining" have a common root (ספר).]
11. See Issue No. 5 of *HaTamim* [for the musical notes, and a history and analysis of this *niggun*].

does one make his "self" shine?' He then immediately continued, in the traditional melody of a [Talmudic] reply: 'This is with what one makes his "self" shine: with "seven complete weeks" — by refining his seven attributes so that each attribute itself will consist of seven; thus, the seven attributes themselves will constitute seven *Shabbasos*, for *Shabbos* itself needs no refinement.'

"When I grew older, and I became acquainted with my grandfather's chassidim," continued the *Tzemach Tzedek*, "I observed that they fulfilled the commandment of 'You shall count for yourselves'; they truly made their 'self' shine brilliantly.

"Our Rabbis of blessed memory tell us," concluded the *Tzemach Tzedek*, "that the Early Sages were called *sofrim* [literally 'scribes' or 'counters'] because they used to count all the letters of the Torah.[12] And my saintly grandfather's chassidim used to count the all the letters of what he said to them in *yechidus*."

---

12. [A play on words: the Hebrew word for "scribe" has the same root as "counting" (and "shining") (ספר).]

Appendix D:

Short history of *Yeshivah Tomchei Temimim*
A general overview of the development of our holy *Yeshivah Tomchei Temimim* of Lubavitch[1]

By
The Editors of *HaTamim*
(On the occasion of its fortieth anniversary)

Forty years (5657-5697 [1897-1937]) have passed since the international holy institution, *Yeshivah Tomchei Temimim*, was first established in Lubavitch by our holy master and Rebbe, Rabbi Shalom Dov Ber Schneersohn (of holy and blessed memory).

The history of the holy *yeshivah* may be divided into two general periods: a) the period when the *yeshivah* was located

---

1. From *HaTamim*, Issue No. 7, pp. 745-747; 12-13 *Tammuz* 5697. This article appeared in the regular column of *HaTamim*, "Greetings to Our Brethren." The editors of *HaTamim* inserted the following introductory remarks at the beginning of this article:

   On the occasion of the fortieth anniversary of the holy *Yeshivah Tomchei Temimim* (may G-d protect and preserve it), we herewith commence the publication of a series of essays on the subject of the establishment of this holy *yeshivah*, its goals, its development, and its founding, from the day of its first conception until today.

   In this issue we present a general overview of the *yeshivah's* development. In future issues we will continue (with G-d's help) to publish various letters and essays which will give the reader some idea of the inner meaning and values of this most precious institution, and of it lofty stature.

APPENDIX D

in Russia, between the years 5657 and 5681 [1897-1921]; b) the present period, since 5681, when the *yeshivah* is located in Poland.

Under the influence of the holy *yeshivah's* great founder, and later under the influence of the founder's son, the Rebbe (Rabbi Yosef Yitzchak Schneersohn) *shlita*, the present leader of *Chassidei Chabad*, the *yeshivah* has grown and developed. The student body now numbers four or five hundred.

During its first twenty-four years [in Russia] our holy *yeshivah* shined with two-fold brilliance: the revealed aspects of Torah, and the teachings of *Chabad*. It was an ever more powerful source, from which thousands of students drew their spiritual sustenance. During this first period, the *yeshivah* produced hundreds of rabbis and *geonim*, expert *shochtim*, and thousands of Torah scholars who excel in learning and in fear of Heaven. Some of them are businessmen, and others are simple laborers, but all have spread their wings in the fields of Torah and *avodah*. The influence of their spirit extends to those around them. They do honor and glory not only to their spiritual source, *Yeshivah Tomchei Temimim* (which raised such distinguished sons), but also to traditional Jewry at large.

The *yeshivah* suffered many upheavals and exiles under the Soviet regime. At the same time, it also suffered under the wicked decrees and persecutions of the *Yevsektzia*. But the Rebbe *shlita* stood constantly on guard, using his utmost powers to fortify and support the *yeshivah*. With G-d's help, he succeeded in preserving the *yeshivah's* existence, so that it could continue to disseminate the Torah and to enroll large numbers of students.

In the year 5681, on the *yahrtzeit* of its founder (whose soul is in *Gan Eden*), the *yeshivah* moved to Poland, where it could expand. Multitudes of students — from all parts of

Poland and neighboring countries — began pouring into Warsaw, the *yeshivah's* new headquarters. They had come to bask in the glory of this famous institution.

The *yeshivah* moved to new quarters several times, to provide the ever-increasing number of students with more spacious and comfortable accommodations. The *yeshivah* also opened branches in several other cities of Poland and abroad. In 5696 [1936], the central *yeshivah* (with its older students) moved to Otwock (leaving the three youngest classes in Warsaw).

Otwock is a famous resort town and health spa, not far from the capital. Here, the *yeshivah* has at its disposal several buildings (each with many rooms), located in a large park with cedar trees, affording a healthful environment. It goes without saying that the fresh clear air and the quiet and restful surroundings, far away from the noise of the capital city, instilled a fresh spirit into the *yeshivah*. This raised the spirits of the students, and it had a beneficial effect on both their health and the progress of their studies.

There are now seven additional branches in various cities, all under the umbrella of the central *yeshivah* in Otwock-Warsaw. The total number of students in the central *yeshivah* and its branches comes to many hundreds (may their numbers increase). They are delightful students, possessing acute mental faculties and perfect fear of Heaven. Whoever sees them, knows them for "the children blessed by G-d."

The holy *Yeshivah Tomchei Temimim* is one of the largest *yeshivos* in the world, both in size and in stature. However, its nature and character as a *Chabad yeshivah* make it unique among all other *yeshivos*: [to use a metaphor,] the orchard is special, the trees are special, and the one who planted it and cares for it is special. *Tomchei Temimim* is not merely an academy for study and teaching; it is also a training facility, where Jewish youth are trained in Torah and *avodah*, so that Torah study and fulfillment of the *mitzvos* may be done with relish and inner vitality, and not merely by rote.

In a letter written to *Anash* on the occasion of the founding of our holy *yeshivah*, our holy founder described the *yeshivah's* goals, to serve as:

> A place where *bochurim* who desire to study may do so, and they may pursue diligent study of *Gemara-Rashi-Tosafos*. However, all this should be under proper supervision, so that the seeds of faith and piety may be implanted in their hearts. Their eyes should be lit up with the light of knowledge, so that they may understand G-d, and know what G-d demands of them: to serve G-d and to follow in His ways. May the light of Torah, *mitzvos*, and *avodah* shine within them, so that they gain merit both for themselves and for society at large.

The *yeshivah* adopted this as its goal, bringing up Jewish youth according to the spirit of the Torah as a complete entity, and the ways of *Chassidus*. This implies that in addition to studying the revealed aspects of the Torah — *Gemara* and *Poskim* — a special session was instituted each day for studying the *Chabad* approach to the teachings of *Chassidus*.

This study of *Chabad Chassidus* implants a firm foundation of love of the Torah and fear of Heaven in the student's heart, through understanding and inner appreciation, and based upon their intellectual endeavors through wisdom, understanding, and knowledge.

Thus, the student's mind acquires broad knowledge and proper understanding of the essence and the inner meaning of Judaism. This also gives him the strength and fortitude to withstand the attractions of other ways of life, without even the slightest deviation from the straight path. Furthermore, through the inner strength of his soul, he also has the power and fortitude to influence his neighbors, and to prevent these foreign influences from gaining a foothold among them.

During the two generations of its existence, the *yeshivah* has fulfilled its great mission on the highest plane. Hundreds, even thousands, of exceptional Torah scholars, *Temimim*, are distributed throughout many countries. Wherever they live, they are recognized for their outstanding Torah study, their piety, and their holy ways. Many also distinguish themselves by serving important and prestigious congregations — in Europe and America — as rabbis, *roshei yeshivah*, *shochtim*, and even influential businessmen who provide spiritual benefit to the public.

Thank G-d, the holy *yeshivah* continues to grow from strength to strength, and the student population is continuously enlarging. Many great rabbis and Rebbeim *shlita* who have visited our *yeshivah* have heaped acclaim and praise upon it and its eminent students, saying that the holy *Yeshivah Tomchei Temimim* is the pride and glory of traditional Judaism in general, and of all *Anash* in particular.

The *yeshivah* also sees to the physical needs of the students: bread and condiments, clothing and shoes, medical care and rehabilitation. The students receive all this in the most honorable way, and in the most cheerful spirits.... [The article concludes with an appeal for funds.]

Founders of Chassidism & Leaders of Chabad-Lubavitch

Baal Shem Tov (בעל שם טוב; lit., "Master of the Good Name"): R. Yisrael ben R. Eliezer (1698-1760), founder of *Chassidism*.

The Maggid of Mezritch (lit., "the preacher of Mezritch"): R. Dov Ber (d. 1772), disciple of the Baal Shem Tov, and mentor of the Alter Rebbe.

The Alter Rebbe (דער אלטער רבי; lit., "the Old Rebbe"; Yid.): R. Shneur Zalman of Liadi (1745-1812), also known as "the Rav" and as *Baal HaTanya*; founder of the *Chabad*-Lubavitch trend within the chassidic movement; disciple of the Maggid of Mezritch, and father of the Mitteler Rebbe.

The Mitteler Rebbe (דער מיטעלער רבי; lit., "the Middle Rebbe"; Yid.): R. Dov Ber of Lubavitch (1773-1827), son and successor of the Alter Rebbe, and uncle and father-in-law of the *Tzemach Tzedek*.

The *Tzemach Tzedek* (צמח צדק): R. Menachem Mendel Schneersohn (1789-1866), the third Lubavitcher Rebbe; known by the title of his halachic responsa as "the *Tzemach Tzedek*"; nephew and son-in-law of the Mitteler Rebbe, and father of the Rebbe Maharash.

The Rebbe Maharash (מהר״ש; acronym for *Moreinu* ("our teacher") *HaRav* Shmuel): R. Shmuel Schneersohn of Lubavitch (1834-1882), the fourth Lubavitcher Rebbe; youngest son of the *Tzemach Tzedek*, and father of the Rebbe Rashab.

The Rebbe Rashab (רש״ב; acronym for Rabbi Shalom Ber): R. Shalom Dov Ber Schneersohn of Lubavitch (1860-1920), the fifth Lubavitcher Rebbe; second son of the Rebbe Maharash, and father of the Rebbe Rayatz.

The Rebbe Rayatz (רייי״צ; acronym for Rabbi Yosef Yitzchak), also known (in Yiddish) as *"der frierdiker* Rebbe" (i.e., "the Previous Rebbe"): R. Yosef Yitzchak Schneersohn (1880-1950), the sixth Lubavitcher Rebbe; only son of the Rebbe Rashab, and father-in-law of the Rebbe.

The Rebbe: Rabbi Menachem Mendel Schneerson (1902), the seventh Lubavitcher Rebbe; eldest son of the saintly Kabbalist, Rabbi Levi

Yitzchak, *rav* of Yekaterinoslav; fifth in direct paternal line from the *Tzemach Tzedek;* son-in-law of the Rebbe Rayatz.

GLOSSARY

All entries are Hebrew unless otherwise indicated. Ar., Aramaic; Gr., Greek; Heb., Hebrew; Rus., Russian; Yid., Yiddish; Yid.-Heb., Yiddish word derived from the Hebrew

> For further definition of the terminology of *Chassidus*, see Rabbi Nissan Mindel, Glossary, in the Bi-Lingual Edition of *Likutei Amarim — Tanya* (Kehot Publication Society; London, 1973), p. 774 ff.; and Rabbi Jacob I. Schochet, *Mystical Concepts in Chassidism*, op. cit., P. 802 ff.

Acharonim: the Later Sages, who flourished after the middle of the sixteenth century

Adar: Heb. Month falling during February-March; in leap years, there are two months of Adar, called Adar I and Adar II

Aggadah: allegorical tales and other non-legal matter found in the *Talmud

Aleinu (lit., "it is incumbent upon us"): prayer consisting of two passages recited at the conclusion of each of the three daily prayer services (*Siddur*, p. 84, et. al.)

Amen!: response given after hearing a prayer or blessing, and at certain points during the prayer service; expresses belief in what has just been said

amud: prayer lectern where the *chazan stands when leading the prayers

Anash (אנ״ש; acronym for *anshei shlomeinu*, lit., "men of our peace"; cf. *Yirmeyahu* 38:22, *Ovadiah* 1:7): cordial term used for the chassidic brotherhood; a synonym is *Chassidei Anash* (lit., "chassidim [who are members] of *Anash*")

apikores (derived from Gr.); (a) one who denies Rabbinic authority; (b) a heretic

Av: Heb. month falling during July-August; also called *Menachem Av

avodah (lit., "labor" or "service"): (in universal Torah usage) divine service, particularly through prayer (see *davenen) and (in chassidic usage) through the labor of self-refinement

Avremke: familiar form of the name Avraham (Abraham)

Az Yashir ("then... sang"); the song that Moshe and the Israelites sang after the parting of the sea; passage taken from *Shemos* 15, recited during the *Shacharis prayer service *(Siddur*, p. 39)

bar mitzvah: (lit., "obligated to fulfill the commandments"): the attainment of religious majority, at which point one becomes personally responsible for his religious practice; a male becomes *bar mitzvah* at the age of 13

bas: "daughter of..."; used as part of a woman's formal name, followed by the name of either her father or mother

Basra: see *Bavos*

Bavos (lit., "Gates": Ar.): the first three tractates of the section of the *Talmud which deals primarily with monetary and property issues: *Bava Kamma* ("the First Gate") deals chiefly with property damages and personal injuries; *Bava Metzia* ("the Middle Gate") deals chiefly with ownership and transfer of personal property; *Bava Basra* ("the Last Gate") deals chiefly with ownership and transfer of real property, and with legal documents

beinoni (lit., "an intermediate person"; pl., *beinonim*): (a) in general *Torah usage, refers to a person whose sins are exactly balanced by his *mitzvos; (b) in *chassidic usage, refers to a person who never actually commits a sin either through action, word, or thought, but who has not completely divorced himself from the potential for sinning, as explained in *Tanya, ch. 1.

beis hamedrash: house of (*Torah) study, usually serving as a synagogue as well; in chassidic circles, the terms *beis hamedrash* and *shul are often used interchangeably.

Beis HaMikdash: the (First or Second) Holy Temple in Jerusalem

Beitzah (lit. "Egg"): a tractate of the *Talmud dealing primarily with the laws of *Yom Tov

ben: "son of..."; used as part of a man's formal name, followed by the name of either his father or mother

Ber: Yid. Form of the Heb. Name Dov; the two names are often joined together: Dov Ber

Berel; Berke: familiar forms of the name *Ber

BH (ב"ה; abbr. of *Baruch HaShem*): "blessed be G-d"

bittul: self-effacement

bochurim: young men past the age of *bar mitzvah, but not yet married, usually studying at a *yeshivah

bris milah (lit., "the covenant of circumcision"): (a); the ritual of circumcision; (b) a feast held in honor of the occasion

Ceruvim: angels resembling young children; relief images of two winged *Ceruvim* were part of the cover of the holy Ark in the *Mishkan; (*cf. Shemos* 25:17-22)

Chabad (חב״ד; acronym formed by the initial letters of the Heb. words *Chochmah, Binah* and *Daas*): (a) the branch of the chassidic movement (see **Chassidus*) whose roots are in an intellectual approach to the service of G-d, and which was founded by R. Shneur Zalman of Liadi, the Alter Rebbe; a synonym for *Chabad* in this sense is **Lubavitch, the name of the township where the movement flourished 1813-1915; (b) the philosophy of this school of Chassidism; (c) adherents of this movement (also called *chassidei Chabad*)

Chanukah (lit., "rededication"): eight-day festival beginning on 25 *Kislev, celebrating the recapture of the second Temple from the Syrian Greeks, and its rededication

chassid (pl., chassidim): (a) adherent of the chassidic movement (see **Chassidus*); (b) follower of a particular chassidic *Rebbe

Chassidus: (a) Chassidism, i.e., the movement within Orthodox Judaism founded in White Russia by R. Yisrael, the Baal Shem Tov (1698-1760), and stressing: emotional involvement in prayer; service of G-d through the material universe; wholehearted earnestness in divine service; the mystical in addition to the legalistic dimension of Judaism; the power of joy, and of music; the love to be shown to every Jew, unconditionally; and the mutual physical and moral responsibility of the members of the informal chassidic brotherhood, each chassid having cultivated a spiritual attachment to their saintly mentor, the *Rebbe; (b) the philosophy and literature of this movement; see also *Chabad*

chazan: one who leads the **minyan* in prayer; the cantor

cheder (pl. *chadorim*): a Jewish elementary school; in chassidic circles, this term may refer to a class for a select group of advanced adult students

Cheshvan: Heb. month falling during October-November; also called *MarCheshvan

chochmah (lit., "wisdom"): the first of the ten **sefiros*, and, on the worldly plane, the first stage in the intellectual process, reason *in potentia*

Chol HaMoed (lit., "weekday during the festival"): the intermediate days of the festivals of *Pesach and *Sukkos, observed as minor festivals

Choshen Mishpat (lit., "breastplate of judgment"): the fourth section of the **Tur* or **Shulchan Aruch*, dealing with laws of judicial procedure, monetary affairs, real and personal property, property damages and personal injuries, etc.

Chumash: the pentateuch, the first five books of the Bible *daven; davenen; davening* (Yid.): (a) the prayers; in *Chabad usage also signifies (b) the *avodah of praying at length, the reading of passages in the *Siddur being interspersed with pauses for disciplined meditation from memory on related texts in *Chassidus; (c) used as a verb: "I am ready to *daven *Minchah*" or "he is busy *davening*"

Derech HaChayim (lit., "Path of Life"): essay on *Chassidic text by the Mitteler Rebbe on the subject of *teshuvah

deveikus (lit., "clinging"): spiritual attachment to, or unification with the Divine

Elul: Heb. month falling during August-September

erev (lit., "evening" or "eve of"): when introducing another word (e.g., Erev Pesach) it can mean either (a) the evening with which the specified holy day begins or (b) the day that ends with the onset of the holy day at sunset

farbreng (lit., "to spend time together": Yid): to conduct, or participate in, a *farbrengen

farbrengen (Yid.): (a) a chassidic assembly addressed by the *Rebbe; (b) an informal gathering of *chassidim for mutual and brotherly edification, usually led by a *mashpia

gabbai: (a) an executive officer of the synagogue or other communal institution; (b) an official of the Rebbe's court, who admits people for *yechidus*

Gan Eden: the Garden of Eden (Paradise)

gaon (pl., *geonim*): a *Torah genius

Gemara: the *Talmud; the elucidation of the *Mishnah, and the discussion of related topics, by the Sages

Hakkafah (pl., *Hakkafos*; lit., "circuit"): one of the seven processions with the Torah scrolls in the *shul on *Simchas Torah, accompanied by singing and dancing (*Siddur*, p. 335)

Halachah: various works dealing with applied Torah law

Hershelle: familiar form of the Yid. name Hirsh

Hilchos Yesodei HaTorah: Laws of Fundamental Torah Principles — the first section of the first volume of the *Rambam's legal code *Mishnah Torah

Iggeres HaKodesh (lit., "The Holy Letter"): part of *Tanya, consisting of pastoral letters addressed by the Alter Rebbe to the chassidic communities

Itchalle: familiar form of the name Yitzchak (Isaac)

Kabbalah (lit., "received tradition"): the body of classical Jewish mystical teachings, the central text of which is the *Zohar

GLOSSARY 203

Kabbalas Shabbos (lit., "reception of *Shabbos*"): service recited Friday evenings before **Maariv* (*Siddur*, p. 128ff.)

Kaddish (lit., "sanctification"): a prayer recited by the **chazan* between sections of the public prayer service, and by mourners at the conclusion of the service

Kamma: see *Bavos*

Kerias Shema: recitation of the **Shema*

kesser (lit., "crown"): in **Kabbalah*, refers to the Divine Light as it exists on a plane higher than, and divorced from, the **sefiros*, though viewed by some *kabbalists* as being the first of the *sefiros*

Kiddush (lit., "sanctification"): (a) blessings recited over a goblet of wine, during the evening, and again during the afternoon of **Shabbos* or **Yom Tov*, expressing the sanctity of the occasion (eg., *Siddur*, p. 201); (b) a gathering, including light refreshment and words of Torah, held in conjunction with the recitation of this prayer

Kislev: Heb. month falling during November-December

Kohen (pl., *Kohanim*): "priest"; i.e., a descendant of Aharon

Kohen Gadol: the "high priest," or chief of the *Kohanim*; he alone may perform the sacrificial service of *Yom Kippur

Lag BaOmer: the thirty-third day of the **Omer*, observed as a minor festival, esp. by *chassidim

LeChayim! (lit., "To life!"): toast or blessing exchanged over strong drink

Leible: familiar form of the Yid. name Leib

Leivik: familiar form of the Heb. name Levy

Likkutei Amarim: see *Tanya*

Likkutei Torah (lit., "collected teachings"): a classic collection of chassidic discourses by the Alter Rebbe, collected and edited by the *Tzemach Tzedek*

Lubavitch (lit., "town of love": Rus.): village in White Russia which, from 1813 to 1915, was the center of *Chabad *Chassidism, and whose name has remained a synonym for it

Maariv: evening prayer service (*Siddur*, p. 106)

maggid: a preacher

MarCheshvan: see Cheshvan

mashgiach (pl., *mashgichim*): supervisor of students at a **yeshivah*, who oversees the students' attendance, personal behavior, and study habits, and assists them with any difficulties they find during their studies

Mashiach (lit., "the anointed one"): Messiah

mashpia (pl., *mashpiyim*): chassidic spiritual mentor, who guides chassidim in the teachings and spiritual lifestyle of *Chassidus*, usually officially appointed by the *Rebbe, by the administration of a chassidic *yeshivah, or by the leaders of a chassidic community

masmid: one who studies Torah constantly, with great diligence

Mazel Tov! (lit., "a good star"): "Good Luck!"; also, commonly used in the sense of "Congratulations!" or a combination of these two sentiments

melamed (pl., *melamdim*): an elementary *Torah teacher in the traditional *cheder

mesirus nefesh (lit., "sacrifice of the soul"): the willingness to sacrifice oneself, either through martyrdom, or through a selfless life, for the sake of the *Torah and its commandments

Metzia: see *Bavos*

Mezonos: blessing ("who creates various kinds of foods") recited over foods prepared from the five species of grain (*Siddur*, p. 87)

mezuzos: parchment scrolls, handwritten by a scribe, containing the first two passages of the *Shema, which are rolled up and affixed to the doorposts of Jewish homes

Midrash: any one of the classical collections of the Sages' homiletical teachings on the Torah

Midrash Rabbah: a compilation of *Midrashic interpretations of the *Chumash and certain other Biblical books, composed in the fourth century

Minchah: afternoon prayer service (*Siddur*, p. 96)

minyan (pl., *minyonim*): (a) ten adult male Jews; (b) a quorum for public prayer, consisting of ten such Jews; (c) a room where the *minyan* prays

Mishkan: the temporary tabernacle used as a sanctuary before the construction of the first *Beis HaMikdash (cf. *Shemos* 25-27)

Mishnah: the germinal statements of law elucidated by the *Gemara*, together with which they constitute the *Talmud

Mishnayos: individual passages from the *Mishnah; see *Talmud

Mishneh Torah (lit., "Repetition of the *Torah"): title of the *Rambam's codification of Jewish law, also known as *Yad HaChazakah* ("the strong hand")

misnaged (pl., *misnagdim*): opponent of *Chassidus, either as an individual, or as a member of an organized opposition group *mitzvah* (lit., "commandment"; pl., *mitzvos*): (a) one of the 613 commandments or (b) in a larger sense, any religious obligation or meritorious act

Moshe Rabbeinu: Moshe our Teacher (or Master)

Motzoei Shabbos: (a) the night following the *Shabbos day

Nedorim: *Talmudic tractate dealing chiefly with the laws of vows and oaths taken voluntarily, and how one may be released therefrom

niggun: melody, usually wordless, especially one in the *chassidic style, used in divine service

Nissan: Heb. month falling during March-April

Ohel (lit., "tent"): in chassidic usage means the structure built over the resting place of a *tzaddik*, and frequented by chassidim in prayer

Omer: the fifty-day period between *Pesach and *Shavuos

Orach Chayim (lit., "Path of Life"): the first section of the *Tur* and the *Shulchan Aruch*, dealing with prayers, blessings, *Shabbos*, and the various festivals

Or HaChayim (lit., "the Light of Life"): commentary on *Chumash*, based on the *Kabbalah*, composed by R. Chayim Ibn Attar (1696-1743), who was known as "the Holy Or HaChayim"

Panim Yafos (lit., "Beautiful Faces"): commentary on *Chumash*, based on both *Halachah* and *Kabbalah*, by R. Pinchas HaLevy Horowitz of Frankfürt (c. 1730-1805), a disciple of the *Maggid* of Mezritch

parshah: portion of the Torah read publicly each week

Parshas ...: the week when a named *parshah* is read

Pesach: the Passover Festival, occurring on 15 *Nissan, celebrating the Exodus from Egypt

Pesachim ("Pesach Sacrifices"): *Talmudic tractate dealing chiefly with the festival of *Pesach, its rituals and sacrificial service, and things forbidden during the festival

pidyon (lit., "redemption"; short for *pidyon nefesh*, lit., "redemption of the soul"): a written note, usually accompanied by donation for charity, in which the writer petitions the *Rebbe to intercede in prayer on behalf of himself or of another person named therein; usually given to the Rebbe during *yechidus*, or deposited at the *Ohel* of a departed *tzaddik*

pidyon sh'vuyim: ransom of captives

pilpul (pl., *pilpulim*): a complex scholarly dissertation

Piskei HaRosh: a compilation of *Halachic rulings by R. Asher ben Yechiel (c. 1250-1327, also known as the *Rosh*, an acronym for Rabbeinu Asher), gleaned from his commentary on the *Talmud

Poskim: (a) works of applied Jewish law; (b) the authors of these works

Purim (lit., "lots"): joyous festival falling on 14 *Adar, commemorating the miraculous rescue of the Jews of the Persian Empire from a wicked plots to exterminate them

Rabbeinu Tam's tefillin: *tefillin in which the written passages are arranged in the order prescribed by *Rabbeinu* [Yaakov ben Meir] *Tam* (c. 1100-1171), a grandson of *Rashi, and one of the leading authors of *Tosafos*; these *tefillin* are put on by *chassidim and other extra-scrupulous people at the end of the prayers, after *Rashi's tefillin* have been removed

Rambam (רמב״ם; acronym for Rabbi Moshe ben Maimon; 1135-1204): Maimonides, one of the foremost Jewish thinkers of the Middle Ages; his *Mishneh Torah* is one of the pillars of Jewish Law, and his *Guide for the Perplexed*, one of the classics of Jewish Philosophy

rasha: a completely wicked individual

Rashag (רש״ג; acronym for *Rav* Shemaryahu Gurary; 1897-1989): eldest son-in-law of the Previous Rebbe

Rashi (רש״י; acronym for Rabbi Shlomo Yitzchaki; 1040-1105): the author of the foremost commentaries on the Bible and the *Talmud; his commentary on the *Talmud* is traditionally printed together with the text

Rashi's tefillin: *tefillin in which the written passages are arranged in the order prescribed by *Rashi; these *tefillin* are worn by all Jewish men during the weekday morning prayers; after the prayers, *chassidim and other extra-scrupulous people remove these *tefillin* and then put on *Rabbeinu Tam's tefillin*

rav: rabbi, Torah teacher

Reb: a short form of "*Rebbe," used as a title prefacing a name; colloquially, used with the name of any adult male, not necessarily a rabbi or Rebbe

Rebbe (common Yid. pronunciation of רבי, "my teacher [or master]"; pl., Rebbeim): *tzaddik who serves as spiritual guide to a following of *chassidim; see *Chassidus*

Rebbetzin (Yid.-Heb.): wife of a rabbi or *Rebbe; occasionally, refers to a woman of great spiritual achievements in her own right

Rishonim: the Earlier Sages, who flourished from the mid-eleventh to the mid-sixteenth centuries

Rosh Chodesh (lit., "head of the month"): New Moon, i.e., one or two semi-festive days at the beginning of the month

Rosh HaShanah (lit., "head of the year"): the Jewish New Year festival, falling on 1 and 2 *Tishrei rosh yeshivah* (pl., *roshei yeshivah*): (a) dean of a *yeshivah*; (b) senior lecturer at a *yeshivah*

ruach hakodesh: spirit of prophecy

Seder Birchos HaNehenin: "Order of Blessings over Various kinds of Enjoyment" — a short treatise by the Alter Rebbe, printed in the unabridged version of his *Siddur, compiling the laws regarding various blessings

sefer (pl., *seforim*): a [sacred] text

Sefer Shel Beinonim: see *Tanya*

sefirah (pl., *sefiros*): *Kabbalistic term for the attributes of G-dliness which serve as a medium between His infinite light and our limited framework of reference, or between the supernal worlds, and our lower world

Selichos (lit., "pardons"): (a) special prayers recited before dawn during the week preceding *Rosh HaShanah; (b) the days during these prayers are recited

Seven-Seventy (or 770): familiar name for the building at 770 Eastern Parkway, in the Crown Heights section of Brooklyn, New York; the central headquarters of the worldwide Lubavitcher Chassidic Movement, the Previous Rebbe's residence from 1940 until his passing in 1950, and the present home of the central *Yeshivah Tomchei Temimim*

Sha! (Yid.): "Silence!"

Shaarei Orah (lit., "Gates of Illumination"): *Chassidic essays by the Mitteler Rebbe on the festivals of *Chanukah and *Purim

Shabbos (pl., *Shabbasos*): the Sabbath

Shabbos Parshas ...: the *Shabbos on which a (named) *parshah is read

Shabbos Selichos: the *Shabbos occurring just prior to the week when *Selichos are recited

Shacharis: the morning prayer service (*Siddur*, p. 12 ff.)

shadar (שד״ר; acronym for *sh'luche d'Rabbana:* Ar., "emissary of our Rebbe"): an itinerant emissary sent by the *Rebbe to visit various chassidic communities, where he collects donations for the Rebbe's charitable funds, transmits the Rebbe's latest written or oral instructions (both to the local *mashpia and to the chassidim at large), and repeats the Rebbe's latest chassidic discourses

shadchonus (Yid.-Heb.): marriage broker's fee

Shehakol: blessing ("by whose word all things come to be") recited over various foods *(Siddur*, p. 87)

Shehechiyanu: blessing ("who has granted us life, sustained us, and enabled us to reach this season") recited at various festive or otherwise happy occasions and when hearing good news (e.g., *Siddur*, p. 87)

Shema: a text consisting of three passages of the Torah, to be recited during the morning and evening prayer services, and before retiring at night, beginning with the words *Shema Yisrael (eg., Siddur,* p. 46; also recited as part of a deathbed confession

Shema Yisrael: "Hear O Israel": the opening words of the *Shema*

shlita (שליט״א; acronym for *Sheyichye LeYomim Tovim Aruchim*): abbreviation placed after a person's name, expressing the wish: "may he be preserved in life for many good days"

shochet: ritual slaughterer, who slaughters and inspects cattle and fowl in the ritually-prescribed manner, for kosher consumption

Shalom Aleichem!: "Peace upon you!" a traditional greeting

Shavuos (lit., "weeks"): festival occurring in very late spring, celebrating the giving of the *Torah on Mt. Sinai, and the sacrificial service of the new wheat crop in Temple times

shtreimel (Yid.): a round fur hat made of sable or mink, worn by *chassidim on *Shabbos, *Yom Tov, and other important occasions; among *Chabad chassidim it was usually worn only by the *Rebbe and his sons

shul (Yid.): a synagogue; in chassidic circles, the terms *shul* and *beis hamedrash* are often used interchangeably

Shulchan Aruch (lit., "the set table"): (a) the standard Code of Jewish Law compiled by R. Yosef Karo (1488-1575); (b) a later version, compiled by the Alter Rebbe

Shvat: Heb. month falling during January-February

Siddur (lit., "order [of prayers]"): prayer book; page references in the present work are to the edition (with English translation) entitled *Siddur Tehillat HaShem* (Kehot Publication Society, N.Y., 1979)

Sifra (lit., "the book": Ar.): a compilation of *Halachah* and its derivation, based on the book of *Vayikra*, compiled during the third century

Simchas Torah: (lit., "the Rejoicing of the *Torah"): festival following *Sukkos, on which the public reading of the Torah is annually concluded and recommenced; observed with great joy, singing and dancing, and the *Hakkafos* procession

Sivan: Heb. month falling during May-June

Sukkos (lit., "Booths"): seven-day festival beginning on 15 *Tishrei, taking its name from the temporary dwelling in which one lives during this period

tallis: woolen cloak with fringes (called *tzitzis*), worn during prayer

GLOSSARY 209

Talmud: the basic compendium of Jewish law, thought, and Biblical commentary; its tractates mainly comprise the discussions collectively known as the **Gemara,* which elucidate the germinal statements of law collectively known as the **Mishnah;* when unspecified, refers to the *Talmud Bavli,* the edition developed in Babylonia, and edited at end of the fifth century; the *Talmud *Yerushalmi* is the edition compiled in *Eretz Yisrael* at end of the fourth century

Tammuz: Heb. month falling during June-July

Tanach (תנ״ך): acronym for Torah (i.e., the *Chumash*), *Nevi'im* (the Prophets), and *Kesuvim* (the Writings; i.e., the Hagiographa); the Bible

Tanya: the Alter Rebbe's basic exposition of **Chabad *Chassidus; Tanya* is the initial word of the book, which is also called **Likkutei Amarim* ("Collected Discourses") and **Sefer Shel Beinonim* ("The Book of the **Beinonim*")

tefillin: small black leather cubes containing parchment scrolls with **Shema Yisrael* and other Biblical passages hand written by a scribe, bound to the arm and forehead by leather straps; worn by Jewish men at weekday morning prayers

Tehillim (lit., "praises"): the Book of Psalms

Temimim (lit., "the perfect ones"; pl. of *Tamim*): students, past or present, of one of the senior **yeshivos* (known as **Tomchei Temimim*) of the **Lubavitch branch of **Chassidism*

teshuvah (lit., "return [to G-d]"): repentance

Teves: Heb. month falling during December-January

Tishah BeAv (lit., "Ninth day of Av): a day of fasting and mourning, marking the date when both the first and second Temples were destroyed

Tishrei: Heb. month falling during September-October

Tomchei Temimim: (a) the **yeshivah* founded in **Lubavitch in 1897 by the Rebbe Rashab; (b) one of its subsequent offshoots

Torah (lit. "law"): G-d's revealed truth, communicated as the Written Law (the *Tanach*), and the Oral Law (the oral tradition communicated by our Sages throughout history)

Torah Or (lit., "the Torah is Light"): a collection of chassidic discourses by the Alter Rebbe, on *Bereishis, Shemos,* and various festivals.

Toras HaChassidus: the philosophy and literature of **Chassidus*

Tosafos (lit., "supplements"): classical commentaries on the **Talmud,* composed by the descendants and disciples of **Rashi,* which began to appear in the mid-twelfth century and are traditionally printed together with the text of the *Talmud*

Tur (lit., "Row"; full name: *Arba'ah Turim*, "the Four Rows"): a four volume codification of *Halachah,* containing *Halachic* rulings of all *Rishonim,* compiled by R. Yaakov ben Asher (c. 1270-c. 1343); the *Shulchan Aruch* and many later codifications of *Halachah* follow the format of the *Tur*

tzaddik (pl., *tzaddikim*): (a) completely righteous individual; (b) *Rebbe

Tz'enah UR'enah (lit., "go out and see [O daughters of Jerusalem]"): a text featuring passages from the *Chumash* and related excerpts from the *Midrash,* translated into Yiddish and arranged according to the weekly *Parshah* and the festivals; originally compiled and translated by R. Yaakov ben Yitzchak Ashkenazy (c. 1540-c. 1626), though the printed edition now used was extensively edited by a later (unknown) author; it has been studied for centuries by generations of pious Jewish women, both uneducated and highly erudite

Velvel: familiar form of the name Volf, a Yid. form of the Heb. name Zev

yahrtzeit (lit., "time of year": Yid.): the anniversary of a person s (usually a parent s) death

yechidus: private audience (more of an encounter of souls) at which a *chassid seeks guidance and enlightenment from his *Rebbe

Yerushalmi: edition of the *Talmud* compiled in *Eretz Yisrael* at the end of the fourth century

yeshivah: rabbinical academy

Yevsektzia (Rus.): the "Jewish Section" of the Soviet Communist Party

Yom Kippur: the Day of Atonement, solemn fast day falling on 10 *Tishrei* and climaxing the annual penitential period

Yom Tov (lit "Good Day"): a festival

Yossel: familiar form of the name Yosef

zabla (זבל"א; acronym for *Zeh Borer lo Echad;* lit., "this one chooses one [judge] for himself"): a procedure for convening a rabbinical court of law to hear a case involving a dispute over money or property; each litigant chooses one judge or arbiter, and these two judges then designate the third judge

Zohar (lit., "Radiance"): title of the classic mystical work from which the teachings of *Kabbalah* are derived